Photography
for
Family Historians

Robert Pols

D1357962

Published by
The Federation of Family History Societies (Publications) Ltd
2-4 Killer Street, Ramsbottom
Bury, Lancs BL9 XXX

Copyright © Robert Pols

First published 1998

ISBN 1 86006 089 7

Printed and bound by by the Alden Group,
Oxford and Northapton.

Contents

Introduction

This is not a book for experts. Nor is it a book that is intended to create experts. But it is not necessary for a family historian to be an expert photographer in order to add to the family archive. There is, though, something to be said for being a thoughtful photographer. A thoughtful photographer is likely to be a modestly competent photographer, and modest competence will serve the camera-wielding family historian very well.

The book, then, is aimed at the researcher who, having accumulated some family photographs from the past, wishes to extend the collection and work towards an archive which plays its part in fleshing out the unfolding story of the family. Researchers who are already accomplished photographers may feel that they are being invited to learn to suck eggs. Others, who are reasonably at home with the camera, may find an opportunity to review their own approach and practice. They will assess the book's information and advice in the light of their own experience. The reader for whom these pages are especially intended, though, is the one whose confidence is limited, who wishes to extend the family's picture archive, and who is not quite sure how best to tackle the task.

It may seem foolish to talk of unconfident photographers in an age when everyone is supposedly used to high-tech equipment, especially since that equipment can often make its own choices and spare us those calculations involving light and distance that were once necessary. But the reality is often different. The truth is that many people feel insecure about using a camera. They are often disappointed by their results. Opening a packet of new prints is an exciting moment, full of agreeable memories and the anticipation of reliving them. Looking through those prints may be a rather flat experience, and after a few such experiences, photography can become something that is left to others.

As for coping with the technicalities, many photographers never proceed so far in the craft as to trouble themselves with such matters as aperture, exposure time or depth of field, but are still bothered by the mechanics of the process. Staff in camera and processing shops are used to people who find difficulties at the most basic level. Customers say, "Could you put a film in my camera, please?" Or, "Could you take the film out of my camera?" Or even, "Could you tell me whether there is a film in my camera?"

So, it is worth repeating: many people are insecure about photography, and many are embarrassed about the results they achieve.

Two things need to be said about this. First, it's not the end of the world if your pictures are undistinguished. The fact that they exist is the main thing. Think, after all, about the old family photographs you have inherited. Those which are later than World War I are likely to be a very mixed bag. But their shortcomings are outweighed by the mere fact that they have survived. When it comes down to it, which is preferable – a selection of artless snaps or no photographs at all? The second point to be made brings us to the purpose of this book. If a little thought can improve the pictures we leave to posterity, so much the better. Whilst there is no point in adopting a lordly sniffiness about imperfect pictures, the desire to do something a bit better is both natural and laudable. This book aims to help the diffident photographer to consider what is wanted and to make a tolerable stab at bringing that about.

To this end, equipment is considered, the taking of photographs is discussed, processing is investigated, and attention is given to looking after the results. If at times the obvious is stated, I hope it will be received tolerantly. Stating the obvious may irritate some; but reading the obvious may reassure others.

Whilst any power to irritate is all my own, any ability to inform may owe something to outside help. It is fitting, therefore, that I should record a debt to my daughter, Eleanor Pols, since I have consulted her about equipment and picked her brain for up-to-date information on processing services. I am also grateful to her for taking the photographs which illustrate this book.

Starting from Where You Are

The existing archive

The chances are that the researcher does not come to the building of a photographic archive empty-handed. There will already be a collection of pictures, inherited, donated or borrowed for copying, and they will already have received some thought. Attempts will have been made to date them and to identify the subjects. They may already be carefully documented and stored, or they may still be awaiting more systematic attention. If the latter is the case, attention cannot come too soon, for, as with other aspects of research, there may still be questions that need to be asked of elderly relatives while there is time. This is not to say that all new photography should be delayed until the earlier examples are fully and definitively accounted for. There will always be problems of identification that remain, and schemes of annotation and storage will always be capable of refinement. But some basic order is needed, for the existing collection is the starting point for any new photography that is intended. Indeed, familiarity with that starting point may be of help in deciding what new photographs are required.

Some of the pictures in the existing collection will already be of an advanced age. You may have a handful of early prints, or you may be lucky enough to have a whole family album of them. However many there are, they are sufficiently old for all of them to be considered indispensable. Decisions may have to be made about how they may most safely be kept, but the need to keep is not open to question.

At some chronological point in the collection, though, there will be such a plethora of pictures, housed in albums, shoe boxes or brown paper bags, that some sorting and selection becomes necessary. Selection does not, of course, mean that those which are not chosen have to be thrown away. It means deciding which examples must be picked out for special protection. After all, the listing of historic buildings or the designation of Sites of Special Scientific Interest does not mean that every edifice or piece of land which fails to qualify has to be knocked down or ploughed up. Family historians are in the business of passing things on, and if what we pass on is obviously considered, significant and cared for, it may (and 'may' is the best we can hope for) have a better chance of progressing further down the line.

This problem of selection arises, in most family collections, at some stage after the First World War, when infrequent studio portraits give way to frequent roll-film snapshots. These snaps tend to survive in greater numbers for the simple reason that they were taken in greater numbers. Since the age of roll-film also ushered in the age of the amateur photographer, many of the examples we inherit fall into the indifferent-to-dreadful range. Indeed, the poor quality of some that we nevertheless retain as valuable to the archive should help us to overcome some of our diffidence as photographers. They remind us that it is not necessary to win a place in the Pantheon of photographic greats in order to create worthwhile additions to the family collection.

The business of selection deserves a little attention. Consciously or unconsciously we are going to use criteria. Consciousness is probably better, since it is never a bad idea to know why we make a decision. What is more, an awareness of the criteria we have used in selecting pictures from the past may help us in deciding what we wish to add in the future. The actual criteria may, to an extent, be a personal matter. In fact, though, those we settle for tend to be pretty constant.

The first four common criteria are firmly people-based. Initially, we look for a representative selection of people to illustrate the individual lines and branches. The number of branches and the importance of twigs will relate to our searches in general. Historians who limit their investigations to the patriline will presumably wish to limit their pictorial evidence in a similar way. Most of us are probably more catholic in our studies and will accordingly aim at a broader sweep of illustration. In seeking a decent picture of an ancestor we may prefer a close-up to a long shot, though in snapshot hoards close-ups are often in short supply. For an important ancestor or relation we may wish to have several pictures, showing the subject at different ages and stages of life.

A second common reason for selecting a photograph is that it shows an event of significance within the family. Christenings, weddings and engagements have long been commemorated by photographs, though in Victorian times it was generally necessary to trot along to a studio to have the picture taken. Increasingly, as the twentieth century got into its stride, the camera was taken to the event rather than the event taken to the camera, and holidays and outings were added to the list of recorded occasions. As indoor photography became possible for the amateur, parties and Christmas celebrations became routine candidates for a souvenir picture. The fact that such events are of family significance is one good reason for keeping images of them. A further attraction of such pictures is that they often show a range of family members, including some of whom few other likenesses survive.

A third kind of picture that argues its own case for special treatment is the one which shows some aspect of an individual's life. The image is not just of a person, but of a person who attends school, works for a living, goes to war, enjoys a leisure activity. In practice, photographs less often record the activity than the possibility of the activity. Little Eric is shown not at school, doing sums or dropping a worm down Celia's neck, but is depicted wearing his new school uniform. Uniforms are often a significant feature of pictures in this class. They are far more likely to figure than the actual day to day business of tackling assault courses, punching tickets or distributing bedpans. Leisure interests may also be indicated by the subject being dressed for the occasion. (And what is sportswear but a kind of uniform?) Items related to the activity may also appear, with the subject brandishing cricket bat, balancing on bicycle or embracing euphonium. Action shots, if they exist, are splendid, but even static pictures, enlivened by appropriate clothing or equipment, say something of a subject's life and interests.

The fourth people-based criterion for selection is often the fact that more than one generation is represented. This aspect of family occasion pictures has already been noted. But special occasions are not always needed for permutations of children, parents and grandparents to appear within the same frame. Such pictures attract because they offer us more than one subject at a time. But they are also about relationships, about links and continuity. In short, they are about the very essence of family history.

The remaining two categories of picture that are often selected are still concerned with people, but they present people in a wider context. The first of these is the kind of photograph which relates family members to events on a local or even national scale. Individuals are members of a community and, from time to time, they are caught up in its life. They may be spectators or participants or even victims. The occasions may range from the parochial, like appearing in a pageant, to the international, like serving in the forces abroad. If it has been captured by the camera, it shows the family member in the setting of society, and will probably be thought worth preserving.

Last in this list of criteria is social history interest. A picture that shows the subject as a recognisable product of a culture or time is readily seen as having a value. Photos of people outside homes, beside cars and in public places all speak of the moment at which they were taken. And if details of the surroundings speak, details of clothes shout. Thus, whilst close-ups may be very desirable for illustrating the line, full-length shots, which tend to predominate amongst snapshots, have their own interest. The fact that such photographs become dated is a source of embarrassment for those who appear in them. Pictures date so quickly that you don't have to be very old to be embarrassed by images of your past self. But for the family historian, the datedness is a major part of the interest. So we retain pictures of relations whose curious clothes are obviously redolent of the thirties, forties or fifties. And, when it comes to pictures of ourselves an equally quaint decade or two ago, we try to be jolly brave and resist the temptation to tear up all but the most acutely squirm-inducing.

Some time has been spent on this question of selecting pictures from the relatively recent past, but the relevance may already be apparent. The factors that encourage us to keep a photograph for posterity may be factors we should aim to include in our own new contributions. What seems important to us in pictures from the past may be just what will seem important to our descendants in the

9

images we create. We may, of course, have additional ideas about our own photography and may wish to attempt things that are excitingly original. But an awareness of the virtues of the archive on which we intend to build could help us on our way and would seem to make good sense.

Reviewing the collection

So we have a more or less ordered and well-kept collection to which we now wish to add. Consideration of the criteria which helped us shape that archive may also assist us in the creation of new pictures. We are raring to go. But let's not abandon thoughts of our older photos just yet. There is a case for reviewing what we have and asking whether there is anything else we can learn from it.

Consider first the gaps. Are there family members who are still alive and who are not represented in the collection. Should they be? Are there any who are represented unsatisfactorily? Are there any who ought to be, but are not, represented at their present age? I wish there were a nicer way of putting this, but . . . . . are there any who ought to be photographed quickly?

What about the closer members of the family who probably already make a number of appearances in the archive? Do the pictures of them meet all the criteria you have used for selection, or are there other kinds of shots of them that ought to appear?

When checking who is represented, remember to consider the dead as well as the living. You may well by this time have gathered together as many ancestral photographs as can be found. But if you have not yet looked into the possibilities of copying, now is the time to do so. Old photographs, that relatives are understandably unwilling to pass into your keeping, may sometimes be briefly lent, so that a copy can be made. If the cost of copies has in the past deterred you from having many made, you may toy with the idea of doing the copying yourself. Of course, for that you need suitable equipment, which also costs money. Alternatively, you need a kind and suitably equipped friend or relation, who is susceptible to flattery and anxious to demonstrate a little photographic prowess.

Gaps in the collection may not only be caused by missing or under-represented people. It's worth asking yourself whether you have, and whether you want to have, any pictures of homes and other sites of family and ancestral interest. Family history photography may be about places as well as people.

But it may be appropriate to think beyond missing subjects and to entertain the notion of missing kinds of picture. Is there a lack of photos that fall into one or other categories of image that you have decided are desirable? Does the archive as it stands adequately represent, for instance, people going about the business of living their lives? Is there coverage of family in the context of wider-world events? If the answer is in the negative, there may be little that can be done, in retrospect, by way of remedy. But awareness of the limitations of the archive so far can make us determined to serve our successors better than our forebears have served us. Put simply, it's a matter of asking yourself what you wish you had inherited by way of pictures, and then making sure that pictures of that kind are available for the period of time over which you have some control.

As well as considering gaps, you might consider faults. More will be said of such matters when the actual taking of photographs is discussed. But if, in reviewing your collection, you become weary of distant subjects with tiny faces shadowed by hat-brims, if you feel a pang of pity for children with their eyes screwed up because Daddy has said they must face the sun, if you tire of telegraph poles growing from ancestral heads, you will be starting to form a steely determination to avoid such things in your own camera-work.

So far the business of reviewing the archive has been a pretty negative affair. But if you notice the weaknesses, you might also try to recognise the strengths. If there are pictures that please you, decide what it is that provokes your pleasure. Has it to do with the positioning of the camera? Does it derive from the mood of the subject? What is it that the photographer has got right? If there are virtues in the collection, they may be virtues worth emulating.

One other positive approach is to look for themes and motifs. If there are any kinds of pictures that recur, you may wish to add to the series. There may already be, say, pictures of fathers in the garden, or grandparents posed with grandchildren, or family groups standing outside the front door. If there's any such image appearing over more than one generation, there may be something to be said for extending the sequence. After all, it has been said that once is an event, twice is a coincidence, and three times is a tradition. Try to spot any family photographic traditions, either established or in the making, and work for their survival.

The Equipment

Cameras

First let me insist that I am not trying to persuade anybody to buy a new camera. If you were thinking of buying a camera with any pretensions at all, you would almost certainly have more than family history photography in mind. But it is true that at any one time there are people thinking of buying or changing a camera, and any readers who fall into this category need to think what would be best for them. Some discussion of kinds of camera might help them to formulate their ideas.

There will be others who have, within the immediate family, access to more than one kind of camera. They may have to ask themselves which camera is best suited to which purpose. They are fortunate to have a choice and it is certainly worth devoting a little reflection to the matter of choosing. One word of warning may be appropriate though. If you decide that your partner's complicated camera is going to be more appropriate to an occasion than your own simple one, do get in some practice with the other person's camera before using it in a situation that really matters. Indeed, I'd be inclined to recommend practice, too, if the choice is a camera that is simpler than the one you normally use. The degree of familiarity may be more important than differing levels of technological sophistication. A camera that your hands and eye feel at home with may well have a better chance of taking satisfying pictures.

Most readers will plan to use the camera they already have and to do the best they can with it. But it does make sense to know what you can reasonably expect of your camera, and to avoid dashed hopes from attempting a photograph that the equipment was never intended to produce. So for such readers, as well as the others, some discussion of the common kinds of camera may not come amiss. Treatment will not be exhaustive and reasonable clarity will be the aim. Readers who fear the abstruse and highly technical are overestimating the understanding and powers of the author.

A camera, however fancy it may be, is basically a box with a hole in one side. When the hole is uncovered, light enters the box and falls on the light sensitive surface of the film that has been placed inside. The film, if you like, sees through the hole and records what's outside the box. Persuading the film to divulge what it has recorded is a matter of chemistry, and the result is a picture. That, really, is all there is to a camera. The rest is refinements.

The refinements matter, of course. They are a number of devices used to control the key event of light meeting film via a hole in a box. First, there is a lens, which is used to direct and focus the light. This may have to be moved closer to or further from the film in order to produce a sharp picture of the desired subject. Then there has to be a means of getting the film in and out of the camera, and, since films have room for more than one shot, a way of moving the film inside the camera is needed, so that a new and unused part of it can be exposed to light for the next image. Next, the photographer requires a way of knowing that the camera is pointed accurately at the subject, so some kind of viewfinder is called for, to give a reasonable idea of what the camera is seeing. Finally, it is necessary to control the access of light to the film. You don't want light getting to the film until you are pointing the camera in the desired direction, so a means of covering and uncovering, or opening and closing the hole is important. But, once you are ready, you want enough light to reach the film to do its work. Since some days are sunny and some are gloomy, it helps if the light controlling system is a bit adaptable. Two methods of control are possible. You can vary the amount of light hitting the film by varying the size of the hole (adjusting the aperture), or by varying the length of time that the hole stays open (adjusting the length of exposure).

That, really, is it. There are different kinds of camera because different cameras deal with the refinements in different ways. Individuals pick the way of dealing with refinements which suits them best, and, for many, the good news is that a lot of cameras handle any complications for themselves, without asking for much help from the operator.

The simplest kind of camera in common use is the 110 camera, so named because it uses 110 film. This film comes in a cartridge that is simply dropped into the camera, so there is no problem with feeding tag-ends into slots in spools. Refinements amount to a winding-on mechanism for moving the film to the next unexposed space, a shutter release which, when pressed, allows light through the lens for the requisite fraction of a second, and perhaps a built-in flash. There may sometimes be a system for regulating the amount of light that is let in, but this, if present, is likely to be very simple. It could be as straightforward as a switch or indicator to be pointed at a picture of a cloud on an overcast day or a picture of the sun in bright conditions. Focus is likely to be pre-set and able to cope with subjects at a variety of distances from the camera. Such fixed focus will not, though, be able to handle subjects that are very near to the lens, and blurred images may be the result of attempts to take head-and-shoulder shots or close-ups of babies.

A further problem arises with close-up shots, since the operator looks through a viewfinder that is quite close to the lens, but not through the lens itself. Thus the photographer sees the scene from a point an inch (or two or three) away from the camera's viewpoint. This can make a significant difference with items close to the camera. Sometimes an inner frame is marked on the viewfinder and keeping important details within that will ensure that vital features are included. But this will not be enough to ensure success with such close-up work as copying old pictures or photographing small items and documents. The 110 camera is, in fact, not alone in its unsuitability for close-up work. Only a single-lens reflex camera, which allows you to see exactly what the camera sees, will be up to the task, and then only with a suitable lens which can be focused down on small, close subjects.

The advantages of 110 cameras are that they are cheap and undaunting. But the cheapness is partly achieved by providing an unremarkable lens, and neither operator nor camera has much ability to respond to varied lighting conditions. The film is quite popular, so high street photo-labs are often equipped to process it speedily on the premises.

Perhaps the most serious limitation of 110 photographs is the size of the negative. Since this is very small, it has to be enlarged many times to make a standard 6"x4" print, and many times again to produce anything bigger. Not surprisingly, the combination of diminutive negative and indifferent lens often makes for an end product that lacks precision. Users are quite often dissatisfied with their results.

The 126 camera, taking 126 film, is becoming less common, but there are still a good number in use. Like the 110, the 126 is a simple camera of the 'instamatic' kind, and unsuitable for close-up use. It, too, is cartridge loaded, and controls are likely to be similarly restricted. It does, though, produce a larger negative, and the outcome of this is that thoughtful users have been known to take some quite respectable photos. Because the format is decreasing in popularity, facilities for quick processing may be hard to find, and many photo-labs need to send the films away.

Disc cameras are also disappearing. The fifteen-frame film for these is set around a disc, which rotates as each picture is taken, so that the next area for exposure is lined up in readiness and there is no need to wind on. Controls are again likely to be simple or non-existent. The tiny negatives, smaller even than 110, do not make for quality enlargements. There was a time, in the 1980s, when people were talking of the disc camera replacing the 110, but that hasn't happened. Anybody still using and liking a disc camera should make the most of it while there is the opportunity. New discs are becoming harder to find, and photographic shops are likely to have to send them away for a form of processing which may prove quite expensive.

Polaroid cameras have the advantage of offering immediate results. Really we should refer to them as instant cameras, though, since Polaroid is a brand name and the company is not the only one to have ventured into this field. Models range from straightforward point-and shoot to more complicated cameras. The special film, which must be the one designed for the make of camera that is being used, is processed automatically. The picture is removed or ejected from the camera with the necessary chemical activity already in progress. This activity is complete after only a very short wait. Most common is the sealed film, where chemicals are contained behind a picture-sized patch on the back of the print. This patch must remain in place thereafter. It follows that there is no scope for trimming, lest chemical leakage should occur. The other kind of film works on a peel-apart system, where, after the necessary brief wait, the coated layer is pulled off and discarded. Film of this kind is more likely to be found in cameras used by professionals for taking passport pictures or used by firms wanting to add likenesses to identity badges. In these cases, a multiple exposure may be made. Otherwise, whichever kind of film is used, there is just the one picture. Since there is no negative, copies and enlargements are not available, except by taking a photograph of the photo itself.

We now turn to the 35mm format. As ever, the name points to the type of film, and 35 mm film can be used in a wide range of cameras. The film comes in a small tubular canister with a tag of film protruding for the user to fit in the slot of a wind-on spool. The negatives are large enough to give good, sharp enlargements up to standard print size of 4" by 6" and beyond, even up to the multiple magnification needed to project slides on to a screen. High street processing labs are routinely equipped to produce negatives and prints within the hour.

The cameras which use this film can be divided into two main groups, the compact and the single lens reflex. Both groups include many excellent models, but they differ in a very important way, which means that they need to be discussed separately.

35mm compact cameras have a built in lens. Some are distinctly inexpensive, with minimal refinements, and few controls. With these it may be necessary to insert and wind on the film by hand. If aperture, exposure and focus are not fixed, they will be simply controlled. A choice may have to be made between pictures of sun and cloud to regulate the entry of light, and focusing may be a matter of choosing between near, not so near and distant. These options may be dealt with by selecting from a group of symbols – a person, say, for near, two people for not so near, and a pine tree for the distances involved in scenery and the great outdoors. Such models perform very much like the simple instamatic cameras, but have the advantage of a larger negative and, possibly, a better quality lens.

At the other end of the range are the all-singing, all-dancing machines which offer automatic focus and an ability to select from a full menu of aperture sizes and exposure times. The lens may have a zoom facility for bringing the subject closer, and there may be a built-in flash which decides for itself when it is needed. The camera may be self-loading, so that you can lay the film in place and leave the working parts to engage the end and wind on to the first frame once the camera is closed. Allied to this facility may be a motorised film-advance system which spares the user the exhausting task of turning to a new unexposed place.

Between the two extremes come all possible permutations of the features already enumerated. As far as complexity is concerned, you get what you pay for, and excellent results can be obtained from compact cameras. But they share a limitation with every other kind of camera that has a built-in lens. The viewfinder does not show you exactly what the camera sees, so they are not suitable for copying or other close-up work.

This brings us to the single-lens reflex, or SLR, camera. This is a camera body with a detachable lens. A mirror and prism system enables the viewfinder to show exactly what the camera sees by looking through the lens itself. At the crucial moment, when the shutter release button is pressed to take the picture, the mirror flicks out of the way for a fraction of a second so that the exposure can be made. For close-up work it is still necessary to use a lens capable of focusing on an object only inches way, but the through-the-lens viewing system enables you to line up the camera with the precision needed for photography of this kind. Thus, whilst in general it can be argued that the camera you are happiest with is the one that will bring the best results, it must be stressed that for dealing with documents, photographs and small items an SLR is the only option.

For most people SLR means 35mm. In fact SLR systems are available for certain other formats. They are available with APS cameras, which will be discussed shortly, and for use with the larger format film favoured by many professionals. If one of these larger roll-film format SLRs is for you, it is probably fair to assume that you already know about them. (If it sounds patronising to claim that such cameras are not for the general reader, I hope I can soften the effect by saying that they are not for me either.)

35mm SLR cameras vary in their degree of sophistication, but will all offer some range of exposure times and apertures. There is, after all, no point in paying out for such a camera, with a good and pricey lens, and then not being able to make it respond to the variety of lighting conditions and kinds of subject that it might be pointed at. Most recent models will offer a high degree of automation, with the camera selecting the combination of settings needed to shed the right amount of light on the film. The camera may also set the focus, wind the frames on, and even rewind the whole film at the end. Some models will allow the operator to override the camera's judgement and make some or all of the settings by hand. Many will require the photographer to set the focus, but this is quite an easy task nowadays. You may have to twist the lens until the picture is sharp or until the two halves of a split image come into line. But the days of estimating by eye how many six-foot tall men could lie between you and the subject, or how many cricket pitches would fit into the space, are long since gone.

A few 35mm SLRs, often ones that have been in the family for some years, may expect the user to set exposure and aperture manually, by turning rings on the lens until the chosen setting is aligned with a coloured dot, or by twisting a dial so that the required setting appears in a window. Even with these manual cameras, high-tech help is on hand to ensure that reasonable choices are made. A small red light seen through the viewfinder may change to green when a suitable combination of settings has been chosen, or a needle may point upwards, downwards or horizontally to show whether the light is, in true Goldilocks fashion, too much, too little or just right.

Whatever the features of the camera, they will take a little getting used to, and practice on unimportant subjects is recommended before travelling miles for a not-to-be-repeated photo-opportunity. For those who find themselves with a camera which requires them to make some decisions for themselves, or for those quaint throwbacks who, like the author, actually prefer to use a manual camera, some advice is offered towards the end of the chapter entitled *Taking Photographs*.

One offshoot of the 35mm camera might be mentioned. Often a very simple item, the panoramic camera tends to be a compact with very few refinements. The simplest models, like the cheapest instamatics, have fixed settings and fixed focus. They give a very wide picture. This is achieved by using 35mm film and wasting much of it. A strip in the middle of the film space is exposed, leaving a wide blank border at top and bottom. The film has to be sent away for rather expensive 'stretch printing', which gives a long oblong picture enlarged from the central strip of the film. A resourceful high street processor could, of course, process the film and trim off the wide black edges that appear, but the resulting cut-down version of a standard 6" by 4" print rather lacks the grandeur that a panoramic effect should create. The processor could always print and trim enlargements, but since enlargement beyond standard size is also expensive, there seems little point. Panoramic cameras have some attractions for those visiting the Niagara Falls, but, unless the clan gathers in unusual numbers or the ancestral patch is one of breathtaking vistas, they are of very limited use for the family historian.

A return to mainstream photography brings us to the Advanced Photo System (APS) camera. Often referred to as Advantix, though this, like Polaroid, is actually a brand name, the Advanced Photo System uses its own film in cameras that have been described as idiot-proof. The film comes in its distinctively shaped canister with no ends hanging out. The complete canister is dropped into place and the camera does all the loading, winding on and rewinding. When the film is finished the canister is slipped out and taken for processing. Expect high street processing shops to send the film away rather than deal with it on the spot.

What you get back is the canister with the negatives inside, a pictorial index and a set of prints. The negatives stay in the canister, which can be sent back if reprints are wanted. Though the canister is always closed when it is in the user's possession, a set of automatically highlighted symbols will show whether the film inside is at the used, half-used, fully exposed or processed stage. The index is a sheet with small prints of each photograph presented in order. It is to this, rather than the negatives, that you refer when ordering reprints, and anyone who has tried to distinguish between two almost identical colour negatives will appreciate that this is a welcome improvement. As for the prints themselves, they may come in a variety of formats, depending on what the photographer has chosen whilst working through the film, for the camera can be set shot by shot to take classic rectangular, a slightly more elongated oblong (HDTV), or panoramic. If required, the format of any picture can be changed when a reprint is ordered.

The cameras themselves are available in both compact and SLR forms. Either way, a fair degree of automation may be expected. After all, camera systems which offer the sort of features already described are not aiming to appeal to the person who wants to treat the choice between exposures of 1/125th and 1/250th of a second as a matter for personal decision.

One final kind of conventional camera, the disposable or single-use item, ought to be mentioned. These are available in both 35mm and APS formats and really represent a reinvention of the original snapshot camera principle of "You press the button – we do the rest". A sealed plastic box, ready loaded with film, has fixed settings and comes ready to use. You point and you click. When you have finished clicking you take the whole camera for processing. It is the processor who removes the film. Disposable cameras can come with or without built-in flash, and there are black-and-white and underwater versions. I am assured that reasonable results are entirely possible.

A product of newer technology is the digital camera. This records the image electronically, so no film is required. The camera is linked to a television set to show the pictures, which can also be downloaded to a PC and saved on disk. Manipulation of images is then possible, and printouts can be made. Electronic imaging is often presented as the photography of the future, and some implications of this technology are considered in the penultimate section of this book.

When considering what to expect of your camera, or which of the family's cameras to use, it may be appropriate to remember that some photographers habitually use more than one. A fully manual SLR, for instance, may allow the photographer to feel completely in control, but a compact or instamatic may be quicker, and therefore better, for snapshots of people. There is no law that says you have to use the same camera every time.

It does makes sense, though, to be sure that you are familiar with the camera that you propose to use for family history pictures, for they are important and, often, not easily repeated. And it always bears stressing that the camera itself is generally a lesser ingredient in good results than the person using it.

Accessories

Flash is a useful accessory for indoor photography, though perhaps not as often necessary as is sometimes assumed. Separate units can be bought to attach to cameras that have no in-built flash facility. Those readers who have avoided flash since the uncomfortable old days of juggling with hot, used bulbs may take reassurance in the fact that modern equipment is electronic and reusable. If a new flash unit is to be bought, the vital thing is to make sure it can be attached to the camera that you intend to use. The best way for the unconfident customer to be sure of this is to take the camera along to the photographic shop and ask for help. Do not buy until compatibility has been demonstrated. Staff in a good photographic shop are informed and obliging people, who will help, advise and show.

The help and advice of your camera dealer may be important to you on various occasions. Cameras and accessories can be very expensive and you have every right to expect patient and intelligible advice. It would certainly be inappropriate for me to comment on any named retailer, but I would recommend the customer to evaluate the service on offer. Perhaps assistants in a shop that sells televisions or vacuum cleaners, say, as well as photographic equipment, are not always experts on every one of the products they stock. Perhaps they are unable to answer your questions or show you the goods properly. Perhaps, too, you would rather buy from someone who knows what they are at. I repeat, therefore, staff in a good photographic shop......

Accessories that are of use for close-up work will be touched on when such photography is discussed. But there is one other kind of accessory that needs to be mentioned, and that is the lens.

It will be recalled that SLR cameras have interchangeable lenses. The camera body is usually bought with a standard lens, but others can be used instead to magnify what is seen or, conversely, to achieve a wider field of vision. Telephoto lenses of various powers of magnification can bring the subject closer. Wide-angle lenses appear to push the subject further away. They thus take in a complete scene that would only partly fit into the field of vision of a standard lens. A zoom lens extends and contracts, telescope-fashion, to cover two contrasting fields of vision and all stages in between. Many start at a slightly wider angle than standard and zoom up to somewhere between the equivalent of two and four times magnification.

One warning is necessary. If buying a new lens, make sure that it will fit your camera. Some lenses fix to the camera body by being screwed on; others, described as having bayonet fixing, work on a slide in, twist and click principle.

Film

Photographers soon discover that there are decisions to be made about film. Individuals become used to particular brands, and familiarity breeds, in this case, confidence. But the choice is not simply about which make of film to use.

Though the tendency in this book is to refer to prints, there is also the possibility of taking slides. That each kind of photograph has its virtues and limitations will come as no surprise.

Slides need to be seen in a portable viewer or projected on a screen. Slides in portable viewers can generally only be seen comfortably by one person at a time. Projected slides can be seen by everyone present, but the room often has to be darkened and the furniture moved. There have been some other developments in presentation methods, but it remains true that looking at slides is an occasion. Good slides, seen blown up on the screen, can be very impressive, and there is something very satisfying about seeing pictures by transmitted light. Even a small hand viewer passes light through the photograph, and a projector paints the picture in light before us. Photography is about recording light, and slides then use light in a special way to bring that record to life. But looking at slides cannot be casual. It is a premeditated, organised activity that may not be conducive to the kind of natural, memory-prompting, anecdotal chat that we often want photographs to provoke.

Prints can be passed round, and two people can look at an album together at a table or on a sofa. Viewing them may be a less formal event. Their physical nature may make them a more natural complement to and illustration of a family history collection which is largely documentary in form. They can easily be presented and inspected in conjunction with text or other pictures. Prints can be copied much more easily than slides, and they can be altered. You can't chop or trim a slide, but such violence is constantly offered to prints, which can be selectively enlarged or cropped to produce the desired effect. After all, we should never fall into the trap of assuming that the splendid frame-filling photographs that we see in glossy magazines all started life looking like that. The best parts of a print can be concentrated on and made bigger, and excessive sky or redundant edges can be lost. It follows, I think, that, unless some lecture or other kind of formal presentation is on the cards, most family historians will generally opt for prints. But whichever is chosen, there is the reassurance, too, that decisions can be reversed with at least modest success. Although in each case there may be some loss of quality, it is possible to have slides made of prints, and to have prints made from slides.

The next question to be asked is whether to go for colour or for black and white. Colour film is accurate and reliable nowadays and it is no longer necessary to remember which make tinges all your pictures with blue and which make confers a pinkish cast. Most people use colour most of the time, but black and white film is still available and can give a very striking effect. If you are copying old monochrome photographs, black and white may seem obvious, but though colour film will not have the chance to demonstrate the rich variety of its palette, it will pick up the warmth of the sepia and off-white tones. On the other hand, colour film used to copy genuinely black and white photographs or documents may end up, when colour processed, taking on a colour cast. In short, black and white film can be useful, if you have a clear reason for choosing it. If in doubt, remember that your local photo-lab should be able to turn colour negatives into black and white prints. So, if you want only one or two black and white pictures, you can use a colour film and have it colour processed. Then, if the black and white pictures turn out to have a touch of colour seeping into them, you can always have those negatives printed again in real black and white.

I have glibly referred to your local photo-lab, but ought to point out that they cannot always deal with black and white film on the premises. If the C41 process is mentioned on the film's packaging, the instant processing shop should be able to handle it for you, and both Kodak and Ilford make C41 film. Any other kind of black and white film may have to be sent away for treatment.

You may have noticed that film speed is something else that is referred to on the packaging. Users of both 35mm and APS cameras will find a range of film speeds in the shops.

Fast film is film that is more acutely light-sensitive than normal. It responds to light shed on it more quickly and therefore needs shorter exposure times or smaller apertures. When describing the speed of film ISO (International Standards Organisation) numbers are used. These have now largely replaced the old ASA (American Standards Association) numbers that readers returning to the camera after a break may recall. Whatever the letters, the numbers are the same for both systems, so those used to ASA have nothing new to learn. The numbers increase by exponential steps, so each speed number is twice that of the previous one, but, in terms of the stops on the camera, means a difference of only one or two. If exponential growth is not a topic you care to dwell on, you might prefer to think in terms of what films of different ISO numbers can do.

The higher the ISO number, the faster the film, and the less light needed. ISO 200 is pretty well standard for a sunny day with some clouds. ISO 100 is fast enough for very bright conditions, whereas ISO 400 will give results in traditional English gloom and will sometimes even allow indoor photography without a flash. Most colour films sold, whether slide or print, are of one of these three speeds, though slower and faster are available.

Lighting conditions are not, however, the only consideration. Moving subjects need to be photographed on as short an exposure as possible, to reduce the risk of them appearing as a blur. Fast film can respond to shorter exposures, so can be very suited to action subjects.

The use of telephoto and zoom lenses can also affect choice of film. These long and heavy lenses tend to exclude light, and the opening of an extra stop or two by way of aperture or exposure time is needed as compensation. Faster film can offset this effect, and the recent promotion of ISO 800 film for use with zoom lenses ties in with this.

On the face of it, it seems surprising that photographers don't use the fastest available film all the time. The trouble is that faster film tends to produce more grainy results. Some photographers so value the pin-sharp results of slower film that black and white film with an ISO rating as low as 25 can be found with no very great difficulty. Most, though, will concede that anything up to ISO 200 will give reasonable results, whilst insisting that graininess is evident with films of ISO 400 or more. Some strongly maintain that such graininess is increased by enlargement. Therefore many photographers will use film that is as slow as they can get away with.

Of course, much of this comes down to a matter of opinion. It may have to do with how fussy or how undemanding you are. Experiment has to be the answer. Whatever the purists say, there are plenty of people who can live with the results of using ISO 400 film. We each have to decide whether we are one of them.

One final point of clarification, unconnected to what has gone before, is needed in this section. The instructions for some new 35mm cameras insist that the user makes sure that film is DX coded. This need cause no panic. All 35mm film is DX coded.

Taking Photographs

Getting started

Before specific family history subjects are considered, there are a few aspects of photography that hold good, whatever is being recorded. It's all pretty basic stuff, of course, but who can say, hand on heart, that they have never overlooked the obvious and produced a disappointing picture as a result? In fact, if a professional's excellent results are so consistently better than the unskilled amateur's underwhelming offerings, this is at least partly because the professional throws more pictures away. The general public gets to see only the successes.

This raises the question of expectations. We, the amateurs, tend to look for every picture to be acceptable. Photography costs money, and people are understandably unhappy if only a few pictures on a film are to their liking. The professional can afford to try more shots and discard a higher proportion of the results. We want to make every picture count, and though we have no hopes of a financial return from our efforts, each picture represents an emotional investment on which we would rather like to see some return. Now it may be that we can learn something from the professional and recognise that there is sense in trying more than one shot of the same subject. But we can also attempt to reduce the proportion of just plain awful snaps we take, and the starting point for that is attention to the basics.

So, why not practise? If you are about to use a new or unfamiliar camera, or if you are taking up a camera you have not used for some time, there's much to be said for getting used to it. Practice, after all, need not be a matter of spending out money on a film, shooting it off, and then paying more money for processing before you can decide how unhappy to be with what you have achieved. One kind of practice is free. That is practice with no film in the camera.

Even before loading a film you can get used to the feel of the camera. Weights vary, contours vary, and operation varies. Get used to the weight and shape of the camera in your hands; discover how to hold it comfortably. Try lining the camera up on a subject, setting such adjustments as are required on your particular model. Try using the viewfinder to compose pictures. Try releasing the shutter and, if the mechanism allows, winding the imaginary film on to the next frame. The more comfortable you become with the camera, the better the outlook is.

Even the business of holding a camera may take some getting used to. The standard arrangement is for right hand to operate shutter release button, winding-on mechanism and any other controls, whilst the left hand provides support. In this way it can prove possible to take a series of pictures in quick succession without taking the camera down from face level every time you need to move to the next frame. For readers who are left-handed the news is, I think, that perseverance is the order of the day. This is a sidist world and photographic equipment is not built for the likes of us. And to be fair I must admit that, though I have fought with fountain pens and suffered from scissors, I have never found the conventional deployment of camera parts a problem.

For taking photographs it is necessary to hold the camera still. In this age of automatic, self-setting cameras, blurred photographs are probably more often the result of camera shake than of incorrect focusing. So, steadiness is all. Camera supports can be useful where there is time and opportunity to use them. Tripods come designed for the purpose. A wall, a chair back, a tree stump or the roof of a car can always be pressed into makeshift service to support either the camera or the elbows of the photographer, and a bean bag can often turn an improbable support into a tolerable one. But for most purposes it really is possible for human beings to work without extra help. Stillness does not mean tense rigidity. It comes from relaxation. Holding the elbows close in to the body can provide a steadying influence, as long as it is done in a comfortable way. If you feel tense, stop, rest for a few seconds, and try again. This is where practice comes into its own. What at first may feel awkward should quite quickly become a matter of custom.

The moment when the shutter release button is pressed is a moment when all the good of a comfortable hold can be undone. Press steadily and firmly. Don't stab or jerk. The finger should move, but the hands and elbows should not. It may help to hold the breath at this point. Holding the breath should, like everything else, be a relaxed thing. It's not a matter of taking in a great gasping lungful, and it needs no bulging eyes or cheeks. You just quietly suspend breathing for a moment while you make the exposure, and you continue thus for a moment after pressing the button. It's easy. Except, of course, that the easiest things are sometimes the things we have to consciously work at.

Let us assume, then, that holding the camera and working the shutter are becoming matters of routine. The tendency at first is to use the camera held in this familiar way for all pictures. But, on modern cameras, the viewfinder is rectangular and so are the negatives. It is natural to hold the camera so that the oblong picture is wider than it is high. This shape is known as landscape format, and is very good for scenery and groups of people. But some subjects, individual humans and many buildings among them, are taller than they are wide. An upright oblong, or portrait format, is what they really need. Hold the camera in the accustomed way, then, still looking through the viewfinder, turn the camera through 90°. (You will need to discover whether clockwise or anti-clockwise is more natural to you.) The appropriate elbow follows up to a position that is comfortable and voilà – portrait format. I do understand that I may be making a bit of a performance of something that is very simple, but it really is surprising how easy it is to go on using landscape format all the time and to forget the other option. I would therefore include trying out both formats in the getting-to-know-you practice I did with any new camera.

It can sometimes be worth getting another person to watch you handling and pointing the camera. They may be able to tell you if you tend to hold the camera crooked. They may also notice points that, except if you are using a single-lens reflex model, you will not be able to see. Photographers have been known to take pictures with a finger obscuring part of the lens, or with the strap of a camera case dangling across it. If you are in danger of committing such crimes, it may be better to be told of the fact before discovering it for yourself when you receive the prints. It should also be mentioned that people surprisingly often take photos with the lens covering cap still on. With non-SLR cameras it really is easy to leave this cap on and not know it.

But holding the camera and pressing the button are not the whole story. In between, you have to look through the viewfinder and compose the picture.

The trick is to look not just at your subject but at everything that is there. The subject is the first consideration, of course. You need to check that it all fits in. A picture which cuts off feet may not be the end of the world, but cutting slices off the top of people's heads is another matter. It should never happen. But it does. So it's worth looking to make sure that Granny is all in. Problems of this kind can arise when the camera is close to the subject and when a compact or instamatic viewfinder gives a slightly different view from that seen by the lens. Sometimes a change from landscape to portrait format will solve the problem, but help may be at hand in the viewfinder itself. Within the viewfinder picture there is often an inner frame, marked out usually in white or yellow. If you ensure that vital details are kept within this inner outline, problems of disparity between viewfinder and lens should be side-stepped.

Look, too, at what else falls within the frame. Is the background more crowded than it needs to be? Are inappropriate details included? Impeccably courteous though he may be, do you really want Great Uncle Albert to be standing in front of a sign which says 'Gents'? Whilst you may well wish to portray Cousin Gerald outside his butcher's shop, are you sure you want to see your own reflection in his window? Come to that, do you really want to see your own shadow in the foreground of the picture? Then there are trees, telegraph poles, standard lamps and the like, which have a nasty habit of slipping in behind people and appearing to grow from their heads. It is remarkably easy to so concentrate on the main subject of the picture that unwanted attendant detail is missed until you see the prints.

Such problems can often be overcome by moving. Subjects, if they are human, can move. Subjects like buildings have to be left where they are. But the photographer can almost always move, and you may be able to cut out the extraneous by coming in closer or by changing your position and viewpoint. With human subjects the moving of either them or the photographer may have to be done quite quickly, before the victims become fidgety and impatient. With inanimate subjects it may be worth roaming round a bit and looking through the viewfinder a few times before settling on your angle.

Remember also to check that the camera is held straight. Uprights in the picture should be parallel to the sides of the viewfinder, and any horizon should be level.

It is, incidentally, worth realising that some problems can be dealt with at the processing stage. Selective enlargements, which blow up only the desired portion of the image, can cut out unwanted background details. There are times when you simply can't get close enough to cut an unnecessary item out of the frame. A telephoto lens might solve the problem, but no telephoto lens is to hand. Selective enlargement can do the same job as the specialist lens. The processing will cost more than routine printing, but it may sometimes provide the required solution.

Mention of processing moves discussion on to working with a film. Handling, composing and releasing the shutter can all be practised with an empty camera. But real photographs need real film. If you are working with a camera that allows you a choice of film speed, don't forget to tell it what you are using. Set the dial or pointer to the appropriate ISO number and the camera will allow for that when setting, or helping you to set, apertures and exposure times.

If in doubt about a picture you have taken, have another go. Indeed, consider a second try, whether you are in doubt or not. If the subject has blinked at the crucial moment the first time, you may have better luck with the subsequent attempt. If you are using a camera which leaves something for the operator to judge, any uncertainty you feel about your decisions can be countered by taking the picture again on a slightly different setting. Whilst it is not always an affordable option to take the number of shots that a professional might, it is worth remembering that something to choose from can be very comforting when reviewing the results.

Consider keeping a note of the subjects you have taken. You may or may not wish to bother recording technical details of camera settings, but you could well need to be reminded of who, what, when and where at a later date. The identity of people will probably be remembered, though large gatherings of unfamiliar extended family members may occasionally cause the memory to slip a gear. ("What was Millie's boy friend's name?") Places can create more difficulty. A week's tour of the ancestral patch can produce a variety of village streets, old cottages and church porches which seem confusingly interchangeable only a little while later. If this seems a little improbable, think of those occasions when friends have shown you their holiday slides. ("No dear, that's you outside that little church in Sienna on the day we had coffee on the terrace with a fountain. No, I tell a lie. The fountain was where we went on the Tuesday.") When it comes to authoritative remembering, notes are favourite.

Finally, there is everything to be said for learning to look over your processed photographs with a critical eye. If this is difficult at first, you could try discussing your results with a trusted and trusting friend or relation. You must be able to trust them to be honest, and they must be able to trust you to forgive them reasonably quickly. But criticising your work is not simply a matter of looking for faults. Certainly you should ask yourself what you could have done better. But you should also ask yourself what you have done right. There really will be answers to both questions.

Photographing people

Everybody takes pictures of people. People are not the easiest of subjects. Buildings don't move; scenery doesn't blink or screw its eyes up against the sun; flowers don't put on a false, self-conscious smile. Yet we tend to agree with Alexander Pope that the proper study of mankind is man, and we extend the idea to include photographic studies. And for family historians people are, inevitably, the most important subject and the first on which to focus attention.

Thoughts about what is wanted must provide the starting point. Influenced by your criteria for including pictures from the past in your archive, you need to decide what you wish to achieve with your new photos. Some fairly close-up portraits may be needed. But you may also wish to show people involved in their own lives. People at work, people at play and people engaged in characteristic activities are all possible.

Picturing people at work may present difficulties. Intrusion may not be welcome. Such factors as safety or confidentiality may come into the reckoning. The lighting of the workplace may be unhelpful. The subject's colleagues or clients may be in danger of finding themselves included in a shot, and may reasonably have their own opinions on the matter. Tact may be advisable, and a graceful admission of defeat may be necessary. But the possibility may be at least worth exploring.

Where a genuine working photograph is out of the question, there may be a second-best option. Pictures of people away from their workplace but in the appropriate clothes or uniform and bearing the tools of their trade may be a faut de mieux substitute. Somebody standing outside an identifiable place of work could be considered.

Leisure activities and hobbies might be subject to fewer restrictions, though indoor pursuits may involve problems of lighting, and outdoor ones, like sports, may require the capturing of movement. Dealing with action shots will be referred to in the next section of this chapter, but again, if all else fails, a portrait of a person dressed for the pastime and holding the appropriate equipment at least says a little about what makes him or her tick.

There are, of course, other situations in which people can be shown living their lives. People eating and drinking are reasonably common subjects, though more often at organised social gatherings than when having an everyday meal or just visiting the local pub. People are often pictured, too, with their animals. A pet can be useful, both because it matters to the person who is portrayed, and because it can be helpful for them to have something other than the photographer to relate to.

There are also situations in which people could be presented, but which we tend not to think of. We come to the business of photographing humans with a set of preconceptions. The Victorians assumed that a portrait must show someone who had dignity, gravity, respectability, elegance, or demureness. The specific qualities might be selected according to sex and age, but, whatever the combination, they represented the cooler virtues. It is true that they were also the more immobile virtues, which was very convenient in the early photographic days of long exposures. But convenience coincided with conviction. Since the arrival of the roll-film camera and the opportunity for everyone to become a photographer, the assumptions have changed. It became possible to capture informality and the fleeting expression. Happiness arrived on the photographic scene and, within the field of family pictures at least, it has stayed. What the camera is capable of and what we value again coincide, and the assumption is that we should smile for the camera. Family photography shows happy occasions and people in cheery mood. To the Victorians a sunny beam might have conveyed levity and lack of character. Today it is an absence of beams that bothers us, and it is solemnity that seems disturbingly wilful. (Reported real-life conversation: "Look at you in this photo, all straight-faced and gloomy. Why aren't you smiling for the camera?" "I am smiling.") Just as our ancestors aimed, in their way, to present an ideal version of themselves to the lens, so, in our way, do we. The subtext is that we are happy. All of us. All the time.

I am not suggesting that the photographer should intrude on family grief, snapping mourners at funerals, pointing the camera at someone who has just been made redundant, or attempting to record a domestic quarrel. It may, though, be an idea to supplement jolly pictures with the capturing of a little ordinariness, covering such humdrum activities as washing up, gardening, reading or pasting wallpaper. And perhaps people could just be doing these things, rather than breaking off from doing them to smile at the camera. Not smiling is not sinful. It is not an admission of a failed existence. Perfectly happy people spend most of their lives not smiling.

The photographs that are decided on will often involve more than one person. Sometimes the reason for taking two or more people is simply that, Everest-like, they are there. Family historians are interested in families, after all, and it takes at least two people to make one. There can be other reasons, too, for taking group pictures. Perhaps that particular combination of individuals is brought together only rarely. Perhaps they form a set, such as three generations of mother and daughter or a complete run of siblings. Perhaps individuals may be juxtaposed in order to bring out a family likeness. Photos of groups, like photos of individuals, can bear some thinking about. What are you hoping to show? Is there some telling permutation of people that it would be good to pass on to posterity?

Deciding whom you want to record and how you want to record them can lead to the profitable use of film, though there will, naturally, also be occasions where you simply respond to people and circumstances. Either way, the setting up and taking of the photographs deserves some attention.

So, you are with your subject. Whether or not you hope for smiles, you probably want them to feel reasonably easy about the experience and to be themselves, so that you can end up with a likeness that seems accurate, natural and characteristic. It is tempting to become a little pretentious at this point and to think in terms of bringing out someone's full character, of capturing their very essence, of seeing deep into their inmost soul. People sometimes talk in such terms when discussing portraits. But, realistically, how many photos of souls and essences have you or I seen? Would we recognise one if it were put before us? Nevertheless, we want to take successful people photos, which may not probe character but which are at least in character, which may not pinpoint the essence of selfhood but which at least show family members being themselves. For this, the relationship between the photographer and the subject is important.

Since we are thinking about photographing relatives, there may already be a degree of warmth and trust between the parties. Even then, a little time devoted to establishing a conducive atmosphere will not be spent amiss. Discussing the aims of the session may help. Indeed, just talking, both before and during the taking of photographs, may be of value. With particularly nervous or self-conscious sitters there may even be some point in practising a few shots before putting a film in the camera.

The sitter may have views on the proposed photographs. If your subject entertains the notion of having a better side, it may be a good idea to respect that notion for at least part of the time. There may be a situation or activity in which the subject would quite liked to be photographed. Again, there is a case for going along with such wishes in order to promote confidence and a sense of ease. You may have little intention of eventually using the suggested poses, but they will help to encourage the frame of mind in which your own better ideas can be more readily accepted. It is always possible, too, that the ideas you are offered will turn out to be good ones.

When it comes to settling on a pose, your reading of the person may be important. A degree of Sunday-best formality may actually be more appropriate to the personality of some people, while others will need to feel relaxed if they are to come over as the characters that you know. Some subjects may be relieved to discover that a huge grin is not obligatory. A half smile or an expression of mildly agreeable thoughtfulness may sometimes do very well. Many will be happy not to have to look straight at the camera. Directing their attention to a different point of focus may work rather better. If in doubt, have several goes. People often feel easier when they know that the picture currently being taken is not the one and only image that they are condemned to be remembered by.

If the plan is to show the sitter in relation to an occupation or activity, it is worth trying to catch them actually doing something. There will be times, as previously observed, where you have to settle for a person simply holding bat, paintbrush or theodolyte. But if they can be using it, so much the better. The ideal instruction is not, "Hold this for the photo," but "Show me what you do with it." Once more, a series of shots may be prudent, and will provide you with the luxury of choice at a later date.

Some photographers believe that children are particularly difficult to pose. This is perhaps true when the child reaches the age of camera-consciousness. Younger children may play contentedly while you reel off a film, or may smile happily at you in a wholly spontaneous and unaffected way. A child that feels warmly towards the photographer will often respond to the camera simply because it is responding to the person holding it. Once a child is aware, though, that wide grins are what is expected, wide grins can be produced with a degree of falseness that even their self-conscious elders find hard to emulate. And every family includes a child that specialises in crossed eyes or chimp impressions as soon as the lens cap is off. Something to look at, something to handle, or a conversation with an out-of-frame third person are possible devices for overcoming the leering tendency.

One traditional way of persuading people, both adults and children, to look animated without explicitly commanding them to smile, was to give them something to say. Rational human beings really did invite each other to say "Cheese!" or, in Victorian times, "Prunes" in the supposed interests of convincing photographs. Perhaps somebody still does. Maybe such an invitation nowadays would provoke a real and natural laugh. I'm fairly sure that the words themselves are of little use, for plosive consonants and long, stretched vowel sounds serve only to contort the lips. I recall once being told by a school photographer to say "Yes", and I suppose that makes for more relaxed facial movement. Really, though, I take the view that not all traditions need to be preserved.

When setting up a picture there are certain basic things to avoid. Cluttered backgrounds and unwanted objects behind heads should be watched out for. These are often easier to escape outdoors than in. Beware, too, the unnecessarily distant figure, a long-established snapshot speciality which reduces the face to something of the size (and interest) of a dried pea. Try to take account of outdoor lighting. The strongest sunlight is not always the best, but it can't be altered to order. It is, possible, though, for photographer and subject to move. It is true that you don't want faces that are lost in shadow. (Remember all those darkened features under wide-brimmed sun-hats that appear in the Edwardian section of the family album?) But nor do you want faces contorted against direct sunlight. Forget, therefore, the old belief that you, as photographer, should have the sun directly behind you. Experiment with shifts of position until you have a picture that is decently lit without inflicting streaming eyes on your subject.

One other thing that may often be good to avoid is the presence of onlookers. If a sitter feels ill at ease, a spectator may not help matters. There are times, though, as suggested in the case of children but of possible use with adults too, when a well-chosen third party can conspire with the photographer to engage the attention and ease the atmosphere.

Discussion so far has concentrated on the single subject, but often the photographer is faced with pairs or groups.

Pairs of people do not necessarily have to stand side by side facing the camera. Like individuals, they may be busy doing something. They may be looking at each other, at a book or photograph album, or at something out of the field of vision. Perhaps they can be posed in a way that suggests something of their relationship. The Victorian taste for showing wives as subservient to husbands and parents as in authority over children has by and large disappeared. The inclination now is more likely to be towards showing warmth of relationship, allowing people to touch or meet each other's gaze. Linked arms, joined hands and arms round waists or shoulders can all show kinds of closeness, and this may range from camaraderie to deep affection, and from protectiveness to mutual reliance. By and large, people know what they are happy with, and it is probably better for the photographer to respond to what is offered than to attempt to impose a degree of demonstrativeness that does not come spontaneously. It is noticeable that people with their arms round each other can pull themselves into some quite uncomfortable shapes, and a little untangling direction from the photographer might occasionally be called for.

There may be a need to take account of the difference between two people's height. If a fairly close-up shot is aimed at, any disparity will be all the more evident, and stooping by the taller person is not much more sightly than the shorter person appearing with no shoulders and a lot of empty air overhead. We are told that short film-stars and notables sometimes act scenes or pose for pictures whilst standing on a box, in order to bring them up to the height of their companion. It's always a possibility that could be considered. A more traditional ploy is to have the short one stand and the tall one sit. This seems a little more dignified and less likely to provoke embarrassment or giggles.

Once the size of subject grows to that of a small group, the potential artificiality of the situation increases. Standing its members in a straight line can be an unintended way of underlining that artificiality. Visual variety can be achieved by having some stand and some sit. Visual cohesiveness can be increased by arranging the people around an object of interest or significance, or sitting them around two or three sides of a table. Sitting arrangements can work well with small groups, and larger family gatherings can sometimes be tackled, for some of the pictures at least, by taking a series of sub-groups sitting and chatting.

There are times, though, when nothing but a large group will do justice to the occasion. Even here a straight row may be avoided by organising the people in a modestly curved line. It is easy for the unassuming to lose themselves behind others at such times. Though sympathising with their diffidence, you may contrive to fit everybody in by varying their heights. Those in front may sit, or those behind may stand on a (very stable) bench. If you find yourself having to organise a number of bodies, you may want to consider whether you can arrange the grouping to make a point. You might emphasise relationships by determining who is to be next to whom. You might use positioning to identify generations. Youngest sitting on the ground, oldest on chairs, and those in between standing could be said to be a cliché, but a cliché may be quite forgivable if it makes the desired point. Alternatively, using rows of different heights, keeping members of the same generation in the same row, and putting children in front of parents, it might be possible to pose a group in the pictorial equivalent of a drop pedigree. Sometimes, though, it may pay to think in terms of arranging those present around a central figure. You thus emphasise the birthday girl, say, or the long unseen relative from overseas, and thereby reinforce the picture's sense of occasion.

When taking pictures of people, whether singly or in groups, there are a few mildly technical thoughts to bear in mind. Portrait format is often more useful for individuals and even pairs, so don't forget that it is available. It is also possible to bring the camera nearer than is often attempted. Even fair-sized groups can be approached quite closely if there is nothing very fascinating about their feet. Head-and-shoulders portraits of a single person can be very telling and can become very treasurable. It should be remembered, however, that most standard lenses will not be able to focus down to a subject much less than about a metre away.

A telephoto or zoom lens, if you have one, can provide a very good way of turning a shot into a close-up. They have other advantages too. Because the photographer is still a decent way off, the subject may feel less crowded. Over-assertive propinquity of lenses can be distinctly off-putting. Children can often be zoom-photographed while they are absorbed in an activity, without becoming camera-conscious and feeling that they have to perform.

Candid shots can also be helped by long lenses, though it is with off-the-cuff photography that the simple and quick-to-use instamatics and compact cameras can also come into their own. This is not to suggest that family historians should turn into paparazzi. Unplanned shots of familiar people being themselves are not normally held to be intrusive, as long as the photographer's aim is to capture spontaneity rather than to cause embarrassment.

If, incidentally, somebody should prove to be really miserable about a picture of themselves, whether candid or posed, that picture and the negative can always be given to them for destruction. It is probably sacrilege to talk of destroying photos, but I think I'd probably be prepared to sacrifice a picture rather than condemn somebody to unhappiness carried into an unknown and immeasurable future.

There remains the question of flash photography. Clearly there are times when a flash offers the only way of making a picture. But it can have its drawbacks. It can produce strong shadows, washed-out faces and 'red eye'. 'Red eye' is precisely what it sounds like. The light from the flash is reflected off the retina of a subject who is looking straight at the camera. The result is glowing red pupils of which Christopher Lee would have been proud. In much the same way, flash can also produce distracting reflections from mirrors, picture frames, windows and spectacles. The harshness of the light and the danger of 'red eye' can both be reduced by covering the flash with a piece of very thin tissue paper. There are other ways of trying to prevent 'red eye'. Since the effect is most likely when pupils are well dilated, some cameras have a double flash system. The pre-flash encourages a contraction of the pupils before the second flash is used to take the picture. The same principle lies behind asking subjects to close their eyes for a while before the exposure is made. They then open their eyes just before the vital moment. After the period of darkness, the light in the room causes the pupils to contract, so that they are already quite small when the flash is used. This method may not do much, though, to help a mood of naturalness and spontaneity. Having people look a little away from the camera is a simpler prophylactic measure.

Flash also imposes itself on the moment in a way that a shutter click rarely achieves. This assertiveness can be just an unremarkable ingredient of a party atmosphere, but it can be more attention-grabbing than is wanted on quieter occasions.

It is surprising how much daylight indoor photography can be achieved with fast film. ISO 400 is often adequate, but films with speeds of ISO 800 and ISO 1600 are for sale. If you have a camera which can accommodate the faster films, it is worth seeing what they can do. Flash is invaluable, but fast films stop fewer conversations.

Photographing occasions and events

Thoughts of photographing groups have already touched on family occasions. There is a long tradition of recording significant gatherings and milestones relating to the clan. Weddings, christenings, engagements, graduations, comings of age, Christmases and birthdays all appear with varying regularity in the pages of family albums. Some of these things were even recorded in the early days of photography with a visit to the photographer's studio. Now that virtually everyone is a camera owner, the complete range of such celebrations is recorded more fully and more often. Only death and mourning, often commemorated by our ancestors, have gone out of photographic fashion.

It has been suggested that giving pride of place to these occasions in the family collection leads to a kind of misrepresentation. Life is not all junketings. Certainly I would argue that the archive should attempt to encompass something of the unremarkableness of life, for that will be just as fascinating in the future as records of major family moments. But the fact remains that such moments are important to people, and it would be churlish not to include coverage of them. After all, when it comes to written records, we are keen to find additional material to fill out the story of our ancestors, but we retain the landmark evidence of marriages and baptisms (and deaths) and are very grateful for such information.

Much of what might be said about photographing family occasions has been anticipated in discussing the picturing of groups. But one or two further thoughts occur.

It can be difficult to take photographs at weddings. The organising and bossing about of the large and formal groups is generally done by a professional who is occupying the most advantageous standpoint. It is often still possible to take some reasonable pictures by standing a little out of the professional's way, slightly behind and to the side. The line of people may be angled rather than facing you, and members of the group will not meet your camera's eye, but the results may not be so much the worse for that. It is not always easy, though, to define the moment when everyone's attention has been caught, when you are not the person who is engaging it. The fact that you are a little further from the group can be compensated for by the use of a telephoto or zoom lens. It is worth, remembering, too, that formal photographs are not the only possibility. Good pictures can be taken of small groups as they wait their turn to be summoned to the line-up, and there is often an opportunity at some stage of the day to engross a moment or two of even the key participants' time.

If all else fails, you can always buy from the photographer copies of some of the official pictures. I don't see this as cheating. You may not have taken the pictures yourself, but the record probably matters more than your pride. You did not take those Victorian studio portraits either, but you do not scorn to incorporate them in the archive.

Another kind of family event is the visit or reunion, when people are brought together in defiance of time and geography. It is not unusual for family historians to visit distant relatives, though such chances may come only rarely in any one person's experience. If making such a trip of a lifetime, you will naturally want to bring back photographs of those normally inaccessible family members. There is one thought that might be added to those which already apply to taking pictures of people. If you are recording them in their own far-off surroundings, is it possible to include some sense of their remoteness in the photos? It may be that they can be shown outside their very un-European house, or in a garden which boasts a lemon tree. The young may be represented as the baseball players or surfers that they possibly are. What can be attempted must depend on the location and the way of life of the individuals, but the idea may be worth exploring.

One other kind of occasion of importance to at least some members of the family is the school photo. There is the mass picturing, now I think less popular than it was, which verges more on a public occasion. But it is also common practice for a professional to visit the school to take a photograph of each individual child. The aim seems to be to embarrass parents into buying copies, since everybody else's parents are doing so. Such portraits are generally quite competent and may have their uses to fill out the collection. It is probable, though, that family historians who buy them are not so much thinking of expanding the archive as aiming, like all the other parents, to keep Harriet happy and avoid Tarquin's tears.

As mention of whole-school photographs reminds us, not all occasions of family significance remain strictly within the family. There may be all sorts of times when one of its members is involved in some kind of community happening. Sports events, public displays and performances, presentations and openings all fall into this category, and you may want a record of the moment when the individual steps on to the stage of the wider world.

Indoor occasions can be tricky. You may be at a distance from the centre of interest, and others may be in your way. The lighting may be too poor for even fast film, and artificial lighting can, in any case, give an uncomfortably warm colour cast to the pictures. Correction filters or tungsten-balanced film can be bought to overcome this problem, though probably few people will do so, unless their need is regular. Flash, of course, can be considered, but it may not be strong enough for the purpose. Its effect may be to pick out the people in the two rows immediately in front of you, without shedding much light on goings-on at the front of the hall. Flash may also be distinctly unwelcome. Where any kind of performance or display is occurring, it can be very off-putting for those who are tense and trying to concentrate. You may be anxious to capture little Lettie taking her violin solo, but little Lettie is probably nervous enough already, without being distracted by sudden strong lights. If the stage is brightly lit, it might be worth seeing what can be done without flash and being prepared to live with the colour cast.

Outdoor events are better lit, but they can present problems of their own. Your distance from the subject can be reduced if you have a long lens, and that may serve, too, to cut out some extraneous matter. Sporting occasions, fêtes and carnivals often take place against a crowded background. Notices, banners and advertising hoardings may, in some cases, add to the atmosphere. In others they clamour for the eye's attention and compete with the real subject of the picture. A telephoto or zoom lens may help you to concentrate attention on what really matters to you. Alternatively, you may be able to improve the situation by changing your own position.

Vigorous movement is often a feature of outdoor events, and, if you have the choice, a fast shutter speed should be chosen to handle it. The longer the aperture is open, the greater distance the subject travels, and the bigger the blur. Movement across the field of view is harder to cope with than movement towards or away from the camera. An exposure time of 1/500th of a second can deal with most human motion; 1/1000th of a second makes assurance doubly sure. If the movement is from one side of the viewfinder to the other, there is another wheeze you can try. You can pan the camera with the action. This means that, shooting from the side, you follow your subject with the camera, watching through the viewfinder the while. Then, just as the runner, rider or cyclist reaches your chosen point, which will probably be the point directly in front of you, you press the button. The temptation to stab rather than squeeze is paramount at such moments, and should be fought against. The theory is that, by using a relatively slow shutter speed of, say, 1/125th of a second, you achieve a sharp picture of the subject against a blurred background. The out-of-focus, streaky background gives a strong sense of speed. In practice, of course, there's a good chance of some blurred arms and legs emerging from a fairly well-focused body. The technique may be worth trying, but the emergence of a photographic heirloom should not be relied on.

There is a footnote to be added to this look at public occasions. Both indoor and outdoor events are often covered by the local press, and the local press are generally happy to sell prints. If you think they may have taken the picture you failed to get, you could visit the newspaper office and find out.

Out and about

Whilst people are the obvious target of the family photographer, little reflection is needed to see that places may be important, too. As part of our research we tend to find out something about where our forebears lived. A natural extension of this curiosity is to take pictures of such places. Whilst we are unable to go back in time to photograph our ancestors, we can still capture something of the world they moved in. How much of a something that amounts to is, of course, one of the things we have to decide.

Homes provide an obvious starting point. But homes exist, and existed, in landscapes and communities. So we may take an interest in the street or the village where the home was situated. The church is clearly a building to look at, for it is the source of records on which we rely and the scene of the ceremonies to which those records refer. But we may also want to check out the workplace and the school. We may wish to investigate the wider area in which these sites were located, and to think about the scenery passed on the walk to work, or the kind of landscape that was being farmed.

Photographing scenery and photographing buildings will each receive some separate attention in due course. But first some observations are offered that may apply to both.

With places as with people, it makes sense that we should record the present as well as the past. In seeking out the family's historical environment we should not neglect its current locations. We might consider photographing our own generation's homes, gardens, offices and social venues. In the pages which follow, however, the emphasis will be more on past. What is said about the general business of photographing places will hold good, regardless of when those places were of family interest. But photographing the sites of past activity brings its own additional concern. The question, simply put, is, "Am I actually photographing something that is at least substantially what my ancestors saw?" The word 'substantially' is probably important, because that may often be the best that we can hope for.

Sometimes the skill lies in cutting out of the picture those details that an ancestor most obviously did not see. Our world is full of cars, road signs, power lines and television aerials, and they may be hard to avoid. Often a slight change of viewpoint will improve the situation, either by excluding the offending feature from the frame or by allowing it to be hidden behind something more acceptable. You can never be sure what fire hydrant or neighbourhood-watch sticker may be obscured behind a bush or a bough in the pictures of an alert photographer.

Changes of angle, incidentally, are not only to be achieved by moving in a horizontal plane. Kneeling, standing (carefully) on a wall or even lying down can all make a difference to the view. An empty plastic carrier takes up little space in bag or pocket, and it can come in very handy if you want to kneel on damp or dirty ground.

Bright sunlight is not always available for outdoor pictures. But bright sunlight is not always the best, since the strong shadows it creates may not fall where you would wish, and since the exposure needed for the darker areas is greater than that required for those which are well lit. Contrasting light and shade can be very effective, provided they are behaving as you want them to. Diffused light, with the sun shining through some cloud, often gives the most even lighting. This may be preferable for the photographer seeking to create a document rather than a dramatic work of art, though if both can be created at once, so much the better.

Ideally, then, you visit a location more than once, and at different times of day, until the perfect natural lighting presents itself. This may actually be possible, if you are taking a holiday on the ancestral patch. If, however, the day of your visit is your one chance of a picture, you take that chance, regardless of weather or time of day. If you are not likely to return in a hurry, you have to make the most of the occasion. This may mean risking unsatisfactory results, and it may mean taking extra shots. In such circumstances it is comforting to know that all but the simplest cameras should be capable of giving you tolerable pictures on gloomy or even rainy days.

Those who consider themselves serious photographers may be inclined to sneer at what they term the 'picture postcard view'. Some buildings and vistas are much photographed from a popular viewpoint, and the better known may appear from that angle in books and magazines and on greetings cards. If originality is your aim, then you will explore alternative viewpoints. But the 'postcard' view has achieved that status because it works. It may be predictable, but it has become predictable because it shows the location clearly and satisfyingly. The family historian may, therefore, see no reason to turn up the nose at the routine approach to the subject. It is always possible to shoot from other angles as well.

Still on the subject of the conventional, one common way to add interest to a scene is to explore the possibilities of seeing it through a natural frame (or part-frame). The idea is to include some feature in the foreground which echoes one or more of the four sides of the picture's edge. A landscape, for instance, could be looked at over a wall, or with an overhanging bough drooping down into view. A building might be taken through an archway or from between two trees. There's no denying that the ploy is hackneyed, but it does tend to work. Such contrivance can add depth to the image and can concentrate attention on the scene that it frames. Extra foreground detail in the upper part of a photograph can also, on dullish days, offset the fact that the sky is being resolutely nondescript.

A common practice, when photographing places, is to include a human being or two. It is argued that a person can add visual interest and provide a sense of scale. I think the argument about scale can be misleading. If something in the field of vision is markedly larger or smaller than one would expect it to be, something to compare it to would be useful. But to those of us who don't actually have to build them and thus worry about the finer details, houses are house-sized and churches are church-sized, whilst landscapes go from here to the horizon. Scenery may need something to give it depth, and for this a human might do as well as a sheep, bush or stile. People like to be photographed in front of things, and as a way of marking territory this has more to recommend it than the methods used by some other mammals. But people are immensely datable. If you are trying to evoke what an ancestor saw, it may be appropriate to keep modern clothes and hairstyles out of the picture.

I confess to a rather puritan approach to the question of people in scenes, but my photographic background has been of the stricter kind. I hope I may be forgiven an illustration involving two members of my own family. He was a keen photographer who could show great patience in finding a distraction-free angle and waiting for a people-free moment before taking a scene. She was used to keeping well out of camera shot and waiting while he waited. On this occasion he was lining up his shot and she, well-schooled, was staying clear. Then he said, "Could you just go over there by that doorway...?" Her heart warmed. "At last," she thought, "he's going to take a picture of a scene with me in it." "...And pick up that sweet paper?" he concluded.

Photographing scenery

It seems likely that family historians will devote more attention to photographing buildings than to photographing scenery. But landscape does offer some possibilities. The view from an ancestor's window or front door, the local scenery that was travelled through, the natural and agricultural world that our forebears worked in – all are potential subjects. So, too, are the locations of repeated holidays or customary leisure activities.

The trouble with scenery, though, is that it changes. It may look timeless, but it is not. Trees grow. Trees fall or are felled. Woodland dwindles, hedgerows disappear and fashions in crops change. Even traditional crops look different without the traditional weeds.

There is often little or nothing that one can do about such changes. Even where trees are being replanted and hedges reinstated, regeneration will take more time than is at the disposal of the most patient of photographers. The odd power line can be excluded from the picture, but no amount of ingenious selection of viewpoint will hide an altered field system or replace a copse. Often all that you can do is be aware of the problem and refrain from taking the most obviously inappropriate pictures. A little research can help. Old parish maps may allow you to establish where woodland has disappeared or how far boundaries and field shapes and sizes have changed. If, after that, you feel there is still something worth photographing, you settle for doing the best you can.

It should be possible to notice and avoid some of the most glaring anachronisms. You can move a little closer and shoot over an electric fence rather than through it. You can take the picture from the other side of the field to avoid the tractor standing in the corner.

If you can choose your time of year, you may be able manage slightly happier photos. A crop of oilseed rape, say, may be disturbingly modern, but it is at its most disturbing when in flower. Plastic-covered straw bales, too, have a distressingly low rating on the historical authenticity scale. Machine-bound bales may be bad enough, though they seem positively archaic compared to the machine-wrapped items. But they are not there for the full twelve months. If returning at a later date is an option, it may be worth considering.

The chances are low of finding, in the right place, the sorts of crops and farm animals that you believe your ancestors worked with. It may be possible in other ways, though, to give some feeling of the kind of farming they were engaged in. If you are able to establish the kinds of animals that were kept, you may still be able to find examples at a rare breeds centre. Similarly, if you have an idea of the agricultural methods that were standard in the area, you may still be able to find them being practised on the sort of farm that is sometimes attached to rural life museums.

Moving back to the subject of scenery and away from its contents, there are one or two points to be made about the taking of pictures.

The sky can be a problem on a dull day, or even on one of those brighter days when it has a uniform and rather pale appearance. It looks flat and featureless in photos and there is a chance of slightly underexposed scenery and overexposed heavens. The resulting dusky landscape under a washed-out sky can be very disappointing. An exposure that is set to do justice to the land features will make the whiteness above even worse. Under such conditions it can be worth pointing the camera a little lower and cutting out the sky altogether. The fields will look better lit for not being contrasted with the sky's pallor, and photographer or camera can get on with judging the exposure needed for the scenery without the sky complicating the issue. This tactic works better, of course, in hilly or undulating areas than in, say, the East Anglian fens, where the sky forms the greater part of the landscape.

Exposure problems can also occur with large expanses of water or snow. I'm not sure that I would expect either to feature very frequently in photographs for family history, though snow could have the advantages of hiding some of a landscape's anachronisms. At any rate, the bright, reflected light from either can fool an automatic camera or a built-in light meter into overcompensating. The outcome can be an underexposed picture. If the camera allows you to override its decisions in favour of your own, you can let in a stop or two's worth of additional light and thereby achieve a more satisfying result. Any habitual photographer of water or snow could do well to fit a polarising filter to reduce glare.

Some attention to the composition of scenery pictures tends to prove worthwhile. Many of us will, at some time, have attempted a photo of a really impressive view, only to find ourselves a little later holding a disappointingly uninteresting print. Scenery can look very flat in photographs. Part of the problem is that the grandeur of real life is reduced to a measly 6" by 4". But another part of the problem is that what we saw with binocular vision has been reinterpreted in monocular form. We saw the view stereoscopically, but the camera has only one eye, so cannot give us a clear idea of distance. In most cases we do not even notice this limitation, but when the pictures are of distant expanses, a flatness is apparent. We need to give the picture a sense of depth by having details at varying distances from the lens. The view needs two or more layers. The resulting photograph is, of course, still not stereoscopic, but we make it easier for eye and brain to pretend that it is. If, for instance, the picture contains a large tree with a smaller tree behind it, the brain interprets the difference in size in terms of difference in distance, and thus allows us to experience a sense of depth. So suggestions about framing a subject by looking over a wall or between two bushes are particularly relevant when the subject is a landscape which needs a little help to come alive. For the photographer, a short walk to a changed viewpoint may be enough to bring half a tree or a corner of a stile into the frame, and that may be enough to give the picture depth. Even a fairly insignificant foreground item can help. Heather-clad moors, for example, can stir the spirit in real life, yet look devoid of interest in a photograph. But a foreground feature as simple as a handful of stones, such as walkers form into cairns, can make a marked difference, especially if shot from a low level to make the most of its limited height.

When it comes to the organisation of horizons, conventional wisdom has something to say. The traditional notion of composition is to think of the picture as divisible by three, and to sort the visual material into thirds rather than halves. Thus a horizon should come one third or two thirds of the way down the picture. We may often find reasons to ignore this theory, and the complete exclusion of horizon discussed above is one such example. Nevertheless a 1:2 or 2:1 ratio of land to air is comfortable to the eye, and we do tend to feel easier with such proportions than with the equal shares meted out by a halfway horizon.

Photographing buildings

The demonstrable associations of buildings with family can make them a very appropriate photographic subject. Actual homes may, in many cases, still be standing, though finding them may sometimes be more difficult than at first appears. Great-great-grandmother's street may still be full of its nineteenth century dwellings, but the present number 37 may not be the 37 she lived in, for the Victorians sometimes renumbered rows of houses. But this simply means that photography may have to be allied to research.

There is not just the ancestral home, but also the ancestral street, town, village and church. After the home it is the church, both outside and in, that has the most obviously strong associations. Weekly visits may have been likely; occasional visits can be proved by the vital records which form the foundations of our research. But a little investigation will often show that other buildings which touched on our ancestors' lives still survive. School, forge, shop, post office, hostelry and employer's house may still be there to be found. Many will now have been put to a different use, but despite changed trappings the shell may be substantially that of the building which figured in the great-grandparental work, domestic management, leisure or, at the very least, everyday consciousness.

Attempts to photograph such places will, of course, constantly come up against the intrusions of modernity. Townscapes can be particularly susceptible to traffic and parked vehicles, though I'm not sure that villages are often much better. Sundays, light early mornings and summer evenings can be the happiest times to work with the camera, for there may be less traffic on the move and those parked vehicles that are the result of the working day will be absent. There will be fewer people about, too. Even such seething places as Stratford-on-Avon, where it is hard to photograph a building without photographing fourteen tourists photographing a building, can be more camera-friendly at off-peak times.

There are some obvious excrescences to watch out for, if you wish a picture to be as little date-stamped as possible. Be aware of telephone lines and yellow lines, television aerials and satellite dishes, modern paving and street furniture. Keep an eye open for undesirable reflections in windows. These can include not only the routine intrusions that you are alert to in other parts of the picture: heliography and unintended self-portraits are also possible. A common outcome of the laudable tendency to limit traffic in old and narrow streets has been the setting up of one-way systems. A common outcome of this has been the fixing of white arrows and 'No Entry' signs close to, or even on, old buildings. Sometimes you may have to settle for unsightliness or take no picture at all. But quite often you can select unwanted details out of the frame. A change of position can frequently prove effective. Or it may be that a picture of most of a subject is better than a picture of the whole. You may, for example, have to cut out the very top of a building to get rid of a television aerial. But even that may serve a double purpose. You may also be cutting out added latter-day chimney pots at the same time. Modern intrusions are not just superficial; they may have become part of the building itself.

If a building has survived any great length of time, it is likely to have had help. Care and attention, not to mention the desire to make the antique more comfortably habitable, lead to changes of appearance. Even listed buildings, which need permission for both cosmetic and structural alterations, may look very different from the way they did to an ancestor. Often they will look a lot more loved.

It does no harm to be aware of how buildings are likely to have changed. In the case of secular and domestic buildings the possibilities include new chimneys, new roofing materials, replacement windows, the addition or loss of bay windows, altered entrances and added porches. Doors may have been turned into windows and vice versa. Railings may have disappeared. You can't, of course, undo such changes. You can perhaps cut some out of the picture, and you can at least refrain from making others the key feature in the composition. Often it may be more a matter of allowing for changes in the way you document a photograph. It may still be reasonable to claim that this is the house where great-grandma lived, but unwise to suggest that this is the window through which she watched to catch a glimpse of great-grandpa coming courting.

Alterations in churches are often fairly easy to recognise. There is always a good chance of a guide book that will help you to sort the visual evidence. In thinking about the kind of changes which may have occurred, it is particularly worth remembering the nineteenth century's architectural taste for extensive plastic surgery. Spires come and go, and wall paintings are plastered over and uncovered. The font and the altar were the scenes of key family events, but are they still the ones that were in use at the time that matters, or are they Victorian improvements? Use the guide book to establish what remains of what your ancestors saw. You can't put back the box pews or pull down a Victorian reredos, but you can at least know what has become different and avoid imagining an eighteenth century ancestor being preached at from an 1876 pulpit.

Given that a church has four sides, there is usually a good chance of finding at least one angle from which an appropriate photograph can be taken. Similarly inside, if the view towards the altar has changed, the view towards the west door may be much the same. A carefully selected long shot or two is often possible. To this or these can be added some more selective shots, offering closer views of some of the details that you can be confident about. Since churches are often tall, a telephoto or zoom lens can be invaluable in achieving such pictures.

Just as professional shots of weddings and public events may usefully supplement the archive, so bought postcards and old prints may be legitimate additions when dealing with buildings or, indeed, countryside. They may offer the huge consolation of depicting the genuinely earlier article. However useful these may be, though, the family historian may still wish to include some personal efforts in the collection. A common function of a photograph is to say, "I was there". Such a claim with such a subject amounts to a spanning of the generations and the creation of a link. It is a case of family significance photographed by family. Thus, since there will be historians who wish to take pictures of buildings in spite of the discrepancies created by the passage of time, the mention of some points of technique seems in order.

Light, as always, matters. The time of day affects the nature and direction of the light. At the wrong time of day the most important side of a building can be shadowed and featureless. Three possible remedies suggest themselves. If you can come back at a better lit hour, a better picture will be there for the taking. If you have control over the settings of the camera, you can choose to expose for the important shadowed areas, allowing the less valued rest to be a little overexposed. If you have flash, you can use that to add light and pick out detail in the darkened area.

Flash also needs to be considered if you are shooting interiors. The question of its use arises especially inside churches, and there are those where it is not permitted. In some churches and other visited buildings available light photography may be allowed but flash objected to. Even if flash is acceptable, it may not always do what you require of it. In a large building it may not reach far enough. Nearby pillars may be illuminated, but ceiling vaults may remain dark.

It is always worth considering whether natural light will do. Thanks, if you will forgive the expression, to Cromwell, churches' interiors are often light enough for photography. In fact, that very lightness may in itself be yet another anachronism, if the church is the one in which your pre-Commonwealth ancestors worshipped. But reduced areas of stained glass may make it easier to take pictures by available light. If, as is often the case, a rather long exposure is needed and no tripod is to hand, it may be possible to rest the camera on the back of a pew, or to steady your own hold by leaning against a pillar. If you are worried about the possibility of camera shake, two or three attempts at a shot will reduce the success rate required for one decent result. And there are those who (an authorial circumlocution for 'I') find natural light so much more agreeable than flash.

On the subject of church interiors, it may be observed that a permit may be required to photograph some of the grander sort. This does not seem to me unreasonable. No such requirement is likely to exist in the case of the more modest, unattended, run-of-the-mill parish church, but a box for contributions to the fabric fund is rarely hard to find. Nobody will object to its use or chase photographers down the road to return a modest donation.

It will be evident that buildings will repay a little time spent in exploring them, walking round them and checking angles. You may not be seeking the artistically surprising, but a little acquired familiarity will do no more harm than with a human subject. Give yourself a chance to consider and select your viewpoint – or viewpoints.

Exploration of the possibilities will often lead you to the conclusion that you can't move far enough away to capture the shot you would really like. For the photographer with an SLR camera, this can be the moment when a wide-angle lens comes into its own. This takes in a wider field of vision and has the ability to appear to move the subject further away. The problem, though, is the possibility of an accentuated parallax effect.

This effect, to which wide-angle lenses are particularly subject, is also perfectly achievable with a standard lens. If you point a camera upwards instead of holding it level, vertical parallel lines will converge, often sharply. The result may look like distortion rather than perspective. The eye is used to perspective on a horizontal scale, but with uprights the visual effect can be disturbing. The solution is simply to hold the camera level. When taking pictures of something much taller than yourself, this can be more easily said than done. Moving further away can help, but there may not be room to do so. Moving yourself to a higher level can help, by removing the need to point upward. This, too, is often not an option. You could knock at the door of the house opposite and ask to take your picture from a bedroom window, but few of us would be so presumptuous. The photographer will do what can readily be done to reduce the problem, but often it is necessary to settle for some degree of parallax effect. An alternative, which can work well with very tall buildings, is to accept and embrace the problem by moving closer and deliberately aiming the lens upwards. Applied to the ancestral church tower or the ancestral high-rise flats, this technique can dramatically emphasise height by making it the reason for the picture. It's a matter of making a virtue of necessity or, as Falstaff more colourfully put it, turning diseases to commodity.

Photographing objects

It is hard to predict what objects any one family photographer might wish to take pictures of. They might include handed-down items in the possession of relatives, which the relatives have no cause to relinquish and which the family historian may wish to have a reminder of. Or they could encompass things of a kind which are known to have been in the family, but which have long since disappeared from common use, such as a car of the type first owned by parents.

Small objects appear ridiculously tiny if photographed by a standard lens, because the camera cannot be brought close enough for them to fill the frame and still be in focus. They will be dealt with in due course. But some objects may be of a fair size, large enough to be recognisable when photographed by a standard lens from a metre or more away. They could be things likes vehicles, pieces of furniture, a valve radio. Such items quickly become embodiments of the past, and the wind-up gramophone of our grandparents' day is scarcely less obsolete than the Dansette of our own (or some of our own) youth. History may have bequeathed us, like Ann Hathaway, only the second best bed, but the best one, and scene of all that lineal engendering, may still be available to the camera in a great-aunt's attic. What may have survived to be photographed will vary from family to family, and the nature of anybody's relic is anybody else's guess. It seems reasonable to ask oneself what might exist.

These largish objects may be treated in much the same way as people or places, and previously discussed considerations of background, lighting and choice of angle will probably apply. If, like a person, the object is movable, then it is possible to alter the position of both photographer and subject. You may be able to choose a suitable setting for it, away from the visual distractions of its current surroundings. According to what it is, it may be stood in front of a fairly plain wall or agreeable curtain, taken out into the garden, or placed on a table which has been covered by a piece of interesting but not overwhelming fabric. I have found that bed coverings can provide excellent surfaces and drapes, but I live in a house where hand-made quilts are always available. For indoor pictures a flash may be the answer, though there can be a washing-out of colour and a reflection from any shiny surfaces. Natural light and fast film will often combine to do a satisfactory job, especially if the object can be set up in a well-lit part of the room. It does not have to actually catch direct rays of sunlight to qualify as well-lit.

If the object is fixed or too large to move, then it can be photographed as if a building. Move round it, check the angles through the viewfinder and notice what appears in the frame as well as the subject itself. Then take the best shot that is on offer. But just what items of family significance might need to be treated like a building? Probably not many. Very large pieces of furniture and, for the very few, statues of ancestors suggest themselves. And I'm fairly sure that, if ever my brother tracks down our aunt's motor torpedo boat (Didn't everyone's aunt have one?), he will need to walk around it to choose his photograph.

There is, however, one large and static object that will often be the target of the historian's lens, and that is the gravestone.

A gravestone may cause difficulties. There may, for a start, be problems with the way in which it presents itself. The surface, which may already be weathered, may also be host to ivy, lichen and mosses. Other, taller plants may surround and droop across it. I think I have to argue against attempts to clean up the surface. There is a danger of doing incidental damage to the stone, as well as to the life forms that it supports. Few of us would uproot wild primroses or pick bluebells. Perhaps mosses and lichens should be accorded the same respect as their showier relatives. Of course, cleaning-up measures may be undertaken in the context of inscription recording projects. But there is a difference between a planned and informed operation, agreed with the incumbent, and an individual let loose on what may be both a historic monument and a site of scientific interest. A little gentle and temporary gardening would seem unobjectionable. It may be possible to bend long grass away and tuck it to one side. It may be possible to catch up intrusive foliage and tie it loosely out of frame for a few moments. Beyond that sort of thing, I have to favour taking gravestones as you find them.

It follows that we may need to think of our photograph as a record of a whole object rather than of a monumental inscription. Such a photograph may still be worth having. The inscription itself can be carefully copied and, attractively presented, may later supplement the camera's image.

Despite the gloomy nature of what has just been said, inscriptions are often reasonably legible and may well justify a picture. In such a case, lighting is all. You need to have the light coming from a little to the side, so that shadows form in the incised lines and make them contrast more strongly with the flat, uncut areas. Sometimes it will help to return at a better time of day, though other churchyard features may complicate matters, with trees, bushes and other memorials throwing their own shadows across the surface that you are trying to deal with. If your flash has some kind of extension arrangement, which allows the light to come from a point a little away from the camera, this could solve the problem. Otherwise, head-on flash is liable to throw light into those very grooves that you want to have in shadow. It may be necessary to simply do the best you can, remembering that a written record of the inscription is a wise back-up to your attempts.

The chance of some degree of success might be improved by coming in closer to the stone and taking a series of shots, each of a different area of the inscription. A closer camera will generally give a more successful impression of lettering. But thoughts of part inscriptions rather than whole tombstones bring us to the topic of photographing small items, and these need close-up treatment.

Spread around the family may be quite a selection of small items which could be borrowed or photographed during a visit, and a picture of which would serve as a very good second-best to ownership. Old photographs fall very obviously into this category, but there are other possibilities as well. Items of jewellery may be of interest, especially highly personal items like wedding rings, or personalised items like lockets or initialled cuff-links. Medals and awards may have survived. Bibles and other books may contain inscriptions, and messages may appear on the reverse of postcards. Letters, diaries and other documents may exist. Anything that bears an individual's handwriting may be thought of value.

In the case of documents, photocopying may create the most satisfactory record, if you are allowed to take them away for a little while. But whether you can make a photocopy or have to be content with a transcription, a close-up photograph of a part of the whole, a key section, say, or a signature, may be a desirable addition to the archive.

With documents, whether in manuscript or print, you have, of course, to be sure that you are not infringing copyright. What may be perfectly acceptable for a letter borrowed from a relative will not be acceptable for material consulted in a record office or for an illustration in a book.

For close-up work a single-lens reflex camera is necessary, together with some additional equipment. Many family historians will choose to seek professional help for such photography, but there will be those who wish to try it for themselves. There are occasions, too, when it is not possible to borrow an item to take to a professional, and when a little do-it-yourself on the spot is the only possibility.

On the front of the SLR camera you will need an appropriate or supplemented lens. 'Macro' lenses can be bought which can handle close-up work, but these may be rather expensive. If you already have a zoom lens, you may find, on checking, that it boasts a macro facility. It's worth giving this a try, by attempting to focus on small close objects, but you could well find the results unsatisfactory. Macro zooms may focus down closer than other zooms, but that may not be at all close enough. Bellows or extension tubes can be bought to move the lens away from the film and improve the minimum focusing distance. But probably cheapest of all are close-up lenses, and these are generally found satisfactory by occasional users. They can be bought singly or in sets and come in a range of strengths. The magnification of these lenses is measured in dioptres (or diopters), and, since they can be used two or more at a time, a set of three or four will allow a good range of possibilities. A set of +1, +2 and +4 dioptre lenses you will allow plenty of permutations and, used together, will bring you to within a very few inches of your subject. If you use these lenses in combination, the strongest should be the one next to the main camera lens. If you are buying one or some, make sure that they are of the right size to screw on to the front of your standard lens.

A tripod, a spirit level and a cable release mechanism complete the list of required equipment. If artificial light is required, investment in photoflood lamps will be necessary, but since a tripod will hold the camera steady and the cable release will eliminate any shake when the shutter is operated, a longish exposure will be no problem. Natural indoor daylight can be used and even a relatively slow film can be considered.

Let us assume that, armed with the necessary equipment, you wish to make a copy of a carte de visite, one of those small, card-mounted Victorian photographs that measure about 4" by 2½". The approach needed for this is much the same as for any small item and, subject to an additional comment at the end about three-dimensional subjects, what is said about copying a carte can be applied to close-up photography generally.

Place the carte de visite on a flat horizontal surface. Screw the cable release into the shutter release button, wind on the film, and set up the camera on the tripod and pointing down at the picture. Some experimentation with lenses, rings or bellows may be needed until you have the subject filling the frame and in focus. Use the spirit level to ensure that carte and camera are both level. When all is in place and any settings have been selected, you simply press the button at the end of the cable. If more than one copy is needed, it is usually cheaper to take extra shots than to order reprints.

Whilst this is the approach that should be recommended, it has to be said that reasonable results can often be achieved in a rather more ad hoc way. SLR and close-up lens (or whatever) are still needed, but cable release, tripod and spirit level can be done without. Using natural light and a fast film in a hand-held camera, you simply do your best. Set the focus down to its shortest distance and move yourself and the camera up and down until the subject is in focus. Resting the elbows on the desk or table top can help you to hold the camera steady. There is, of course, plenty of room for mistakes: you may not have the camera held quite level, or it may move very slightly as you press the button. So, by way of insurance policy, you take every subject twice, and three times if you are a pessimist. This informal method can produce surprisingly bearable results, though one person's bearable is, admittedly, another person's poison. For what it's worth, I choose to use a tripod and associated trimmings where at all convenient, and copying photos on a table or desk comes under the heading of convenient. If I am out for a walk, though, and decide to photograph a flower, I go for the hand-held option and generally find I can live with the outcome.

Whichever method is used, there are one or two additional points to be made.

Watch out for the camera strap when pointing the camera downwards. It is very easy to let this, or a strand of long hair, dangle and fall across the lens.

If in any kind of doubt, don't fill the frame to the very edges with important detail. Even with an SLR, if your head is a fraction tilted, you may be seeing something slightly different from the camera. There is also a tendency for printing machines to cut off a very narrow border all round the picture. So it can be worth playing safe and making sure that everything vital is well within the frame. You can reassure yourself with the thought that the print can always be trimmed down.

When copying sepia photos, use colour film. You won't have the advantage of the full range of hues that it can represent, but it will capture the warm tones of your original in a way that black and white film just can't. It is worth mentioning to your processor, though, that a film consists entirely of monochrome copies. The first reason for this is one of kindness. You may save the processor a moment of panic, wondering what could be wrong with a machine that has apparently stopped using its full palette. The second reason is a little more technical. Colour negatives of monochrome subjects can be very contrasty, so the processor, if forewarned, may choose to step up the density at the printing stage, in order to achieve a better end-product.

Sometimes the background will need thought. You may choose to fill the frame with an oblong subject such as a carte de visite, but some background will certainly show in pictures of items like lockets or rings. Fabric, leather and attractively grained wood can prove very effective surfaces on which to place an object. I have found the covers of old, leather-bound books look very agreeable. If you use fabric, it is probably wise to select something that is fine textured to start with, as the weave will be enlarged and coarsened in the picture.

Finally, be aware that focusing can be a sensitive matter in close-up work. With a three dimensional object, even such a relatively flat three-dimensional object as a piece of jewellery, it is possible for one part to be in focus and another part, at a very slightly different distance from the lens, to be out. Make sure, then, that you focus on the vital image, inscription or other detail, so that if any part is fuzzily rendered, it is a part that is of subsidiary interest.

Being in control

Most historian/photographers will probably have no need to worry about the settings on a camera. Many will be using fully automatic cameras, and will have to make no decisions about focus or exposure. A few will have chosen their camera because they prefer to take control themselves, and they will already be familiar with what they have to do with it. There will be those, however, who are working with an old camera of which they have never really got the hang. There will be others whose camera offers the option of manual override and who may occasionally wish to exercise that option. An automatic camera may sometimes use its flash where you would have preferred it not to. And in special lighting situations, like snow or sunsets, what seems a logical setting to the camera may not be what you actually want. So the ability to override the camera's automatic systems and to adjust settings by hand can be useful. This section is offered, therefore, for those who may sometimes need to think about controlling the camera.

The first control to mention is the film speed indicator, and what needs to be said is simply a repetition of what has been said before: don't forget to set it to point to or show the ISO speed of the film you are using.

Focusing will detain us a little longer. Focusing is a matter of adjusting the lens to the distance between it and its subject. The lens usually has a focusing ring, which is marked with a series of distances in metres, or feet, or both. A standard lens may be marked in stages from about half a metre up to infinity. (Infinity is the setting used for all distances above the highest number of metres or feet marked on the ring.) The idea is to bring the appropriate distance into line with a fixed symbol, often a red line or arrow. So if your subject is five metres away, you twist the ring, thereby moving the lens, until the figure 5 is lined up against the fixed mark. In the past this meant estimating distances by pacing them out, or imagining how many people of a given height could lie down end to end between photographer and subject. Now even a manual camera is likely to do the measuring for you. If you look through the viewfinder and turn the ring, you will be able to see when the lens has reached the right position. The centre of the viewfinder may have a small panel which turns from fuzzy to clear at the appropriate moment. There may be a split image, the two halves of which come into alignment. Whatever device is used, it will be a visual one, so that you can see that your image is in sharp focus.

Though even manual focusing is usually camera-assisted, there are a couple of things for the human being to remember.

If you wear spectacles, keep them on. It may be that habitual binocular-users are accustomed to removing their glasses or pushing them up on the forehead, but this habit should not be transferred to camera use. You can adjust binoculars to cater for the eccentricities of your own eyes. You must adjust the camera to cater for the eye of its own lens, and that eye sees things accurately. You, therefore, need to see as the lens sees. That means that optically impaired photographers must look through the viewfinder with corrected vision.

It is vital to focus on the important part of your picture. If, say, Cousin Albert is in the garden, make sure that you are concentrating on getting his face into focus rather than the rose bush a couple of yards behind. A person's eyes are a good point to focus on.

Autofocus cameras can sometimes cause problems if the key subject is a little off-centre. They tend to focus on the central object in view. If, artistically, you decide to place your person a bit to one side, the camera may set itself to the scenery behind. Similarly, if you are taking a picture of two people side by side, an autofocus camera is quite capable of focusing on the wall that can be seen between their heads in the centre of the frame. Some autofocus cameras have a device which allows you to focus on the key feature in the middle of the viewfinder and then hold that setting while you move the camera slightly to achieve the composition you really want. With manual cameras you can focus and then move the camera slightly, without having to operate any override mechanism.

Care to focus on the right detail is important because the camera may not be able to maintain sharp focus at the same time on two objects at different distances. Any one shot will have its own depth of field or range of distances within which things are in focus. It may be, given a particular setting of the controls, that everything between eight and twelve feet away is in focus, but closer or more distant objects are not. You will have seen this phenomenon made use of on film or television, where the focus is changed mid-shot, as the dialogue passes from the person in the room to the person in the doorway, or as the blurred background behind two blithely chatting voyagers becomes sharp to reveal that the lifebelt on the wall is labelled SS Titanic. Or you may have found for yourself, using a long lens at the zoo, that if you are close to the wire of the cage and the animal is some distance away, you can focus on the creature while the mesh becomes so blurred that it even seems to disappear and you end up with a shot in which there seems, at least at first glance, to be no barrier between the two of you.

There will be times when it is useful to try for maximum depth of field, in order to bring two layers of a scene into focus, or to minimise depth of field, in the hope of blurring unwanted background details. This will be returned to when aperture is discussed.

The controls which remain to be considered are those which regulate the amount of light reaching the film. Light can be controlled by varying the time that the shutter is open and by varying the size of hole through which it passes. A successful picture may depend on the photographer balancing out the implications of these two different kinds of setting.

Shutter speed may be controlled by another ring on the lens or by a device on the body of the camera which can be clicked, slid or turned to the appropriate setting. The speed is measured in the fractions of a second for which the shutter stays open. It is usually the bottom figure of the fraction that is marked on the camera control, so 125 designates 1/125th of a second rather than a little over two minutes. The longer the shutter remains open, the more light gets in. But the longer it is open, the longer the subject needs to stay still. Buildings can stay still for longer than people. So, in theory, can scenery, but on a windy day parts of it are likely to be in motion and require a faster shutter speed. For action shots, as suggested earlier, a speed of 1/500th of a second is generally adequate, though many cameras can offer even shorter exposures. Pictures of people at rest can generally be managed with 1/125th or even 1/60th of a second. The faster speed may be better for children or for other subjects liable to fidget. It is often said that for exposures of longer than 1/60th a tripod or other rest is necessary to avoid camera-shake. In practice, you may find that your hand is steady enough to get away with shots at 1/30th of a second.

The size of the hole through which light passes is dealt with by the aperture control. This generally takes the form of a lens-ring, though older non-SLR cameras may have a slide or lever on the body itself. The aperture is measured in f/stops, which commonly, on a standard lens, range from around f/2 or f/2.8 to f/16 or f/22. The highest number represents the smallest aperture. (This may seem strange, but you soon get used to it.) The larger the aperture, the more shallow is the depth of field. This can give the photographer something of the control mentioned previously. A low f/stop may enable you to render a distracting background out of focus, and a high f/stop will increase the depth of field and allow differently-distanced details to appear sharp. Some cameras have a depth of field scale or preview device, which will allow you to judge how clearly focused objects behind and in front of the main subject will appear in the eventual photograph.

The fully manual camera allows the photographer to adjust both aperture and shutter speed. The fully automatic camera takes care of both. But some automatic or semi-automatic cameras have provision for the operator to take control of at least one of the settings.

In the past it was necessary to judge by eye how bright the light was, and to set in a combination of shutter speed and aperture size accordingly. Then light meters became available, and the photographer would point one at the scene, take a reading, and adjust the settings as the meter suggested. Nowadays light meters are built into the better cameras. Automatic cameras set themselves to the light reading. Manual cameras generally offer aids for the photographer to get the setting right. Lights may be visible in the viewfinder, and these may change from red to green when the photographer has adjusted the controls to the point at which enough light will be let in. Or a needle may appear in view, pointing upwards to indicate too much light, pointing downwards for too little, and settling horizontally when the exposure is correct. The photographer can set in the shutter speed first, if that is more important to the subject, and fiddle with the aperture control until the viewfinder device gives the go-ahead; or the aperture may be chosen and the shutter speed experimented with until the right combination is found.

A degree of user control can be very useful when dealing with pictures which have contrasting areas of light and shade. If the shaded area is important, use that to establish the setting required, allowing the brighter and less important area to become a little over-exposed.

Whilst users of automatic cameras may usually be content to let the technology look after itself, there may come a time when growing confidence encourages them to explore any override features that are provided, to see how they can improve the results themselves.

Picture Gallery

The idea of this section is to look at a few photographs and comment on them. They have been taken expressly to illustrate this book and, since a major aim is to show some common problems and mistakes, a prefatory word is needed. The photographer's brief included a request to illustrate a variety of errors which she would otherwise studiously avoid. I therefore owe it to her to assert that, in normal circumstances, she is wholly aware of which end of a camera is up.

Figure 1 presents us with that popular favourite – object growing out of subject's head. In this case the object is an ironing board, and its presence is rather a pity, since it intrudes on quite an agreeable portrait. It's fairly close, it's cheery, and, ironing board apart, it's set against an undistracting background. It does, though, demonstrate some of the problems that are associated with flash. A reflection can be seen in both spectacle lenses and the shadow is very harsh. Like nearly all the illustrations used in this section, the picture was taken on ISO 400 film, using a fully manual single-lens reflex camera. A zoom lens was used to achieve a fairly close-up image without crowding the subject. This is a useful device, since the closer the camera approaches, the more likely the subject is to feel uneasy. A zoom lens can give the effect of reducing the distance between the two without either of them actually moving. The light switch and the out-of-true vertical to the left of the picture could be trimmed out without losing more than the young man's right shoulder.

Flash has also been used for Figure 2, and hard shadows are one result. There is also some reflection from the wood in the background, and it is worth noticing that glass is not the only material to bounce light back. Portrait format has been chosen, sensibly enough, since it does tend to be useful for portraits. It might have been an idea to capitalise on the format and bring the camera closer. This would eliminate some of the rather distracting background, with its clutter of furniture and half a human being. The girl has a bunch of flowers growing from her head. This is perhaps prettier than an ironing board and probably less painful, but an absence of flowers would have been preferable. The child has reached an age where she feels a little uncomfortable with the camera. She is trying to look friendly, but there is a stiffness of pose which it would have been satisfying to dispel. It might have been a good idea to engage her attention by giving her something to do or something to look at.

The subject of Figure 3 does have something to do. This is, in fact, an example of a portrait at work, a category of picture which has much to recommend it, but which cannot always be explored. The woman, working in a film processing shop,

Figure 1

Figure 2

is extracting the tongue of a film from its light-tight cassette prior to developing. The shop is situated on a corner and has windows on two sides, so it was possible to use available light and put the flash unit aside. The result is softer and pleasanter lighting. In spite of the indoor subject, the use of fast film allowed an exposure of 1/250th of a second to be used. To achieve this speed, an aperture of f/2.8 had to be selected. The machinery behind the subject may be a little distracting, but it could not have been moved. The limited depth of field, which results from a wide aperture, has made the background items a little out of focus, with the pleasing result that they clamour less for our attention. The strip light at the top of the picture is no great attraction. It could easily be trimmed off, though, and that is precisely what I would do before displaying this picture or putting it in an album.

Figure 4 is the first of two close-up portraits taken by flash and using a zoom lens. On this occasion the flash has not reflected from the spectacles, though it may be giving extra definition to the rims. The strong shadow and dark sweater throw almost all the attention on the face. The books on the shelf behind do catch the eye to a degree, but the modest depth of field that results from the f/8 setting means that they are not in sharp focus. The subject looks towards the camera but has been persuaded not to smile at it, and the steady gaze works well. The photographer was asked to provide a selection of variously unsatisfying pictures, but some photographic virtues were allowed to offset the vices. This seems to me to enjoy the virtue of success.

I also like Figure 5. Once again the zoom lens has allowed unobtrusive closeness, and once again flash photography has failed to do its worst. The face is comfortably lit, the shadows are more emphatic than grotesque, and the spectacle lenses have been spared. There is some highlighting of buttons, bracelet and chin, and the arm, being closer to the light source than the face, is paler, but these are small prices to pay for the naturalness of the pose. The subject is at ease, chatting to out-of-frame friends. There is no forcing of a grin for the camera, but a natural smile is the product of her enjoyment of the company and conversation. What comes over especially to me is the sense of listening in a portrait that demonstrates the possibility of being relaxed and intent at the same time. The background of curtain, bottom of a picture and part of a lamp are not what one would choose, but, in this situation, they are clearly what one would put up with. A change of position would have broken the mood.

So with Figure 6 it's back to less happy results. The flash on this occasion has been too strong for the two girls who are the subject, and it has washed out their faces, leaving them with a currant-eyed snowman look. This is unfortunate, as the smiles appear unforced, though the show of sisterly affection has led to an uncomfortable amount of neck-bending from the taller of the two. Not only has the flash worked its wicked way with the girls' features, but it has also been very successful in illuminating and drawing attention to a distractingly busy

Figure 3

Figure 4

Figure 5

Figure 6

background. This is a case where it might be worth inviting the processor to see if the picture could be printed out a bit darker. If that were possible, it could be of benefit to both wanted faces and unwanted bystanders. It all depends on the negative, though, for the most careful printing cannot reinstate details that were never there in the first place. This print, incidentally, is one of only two illustrations for which the manual SLR was not used. The camera was a good quality, fully automatic 35mm compact, which makes its own decisions about the occasions and settings for flash photography.

The couple in Figure 7 have been more kindly treated. They have been taken outside and pleasantly placed in front of foliage. Their faces are modelled by natural light, which was strong enough to allow a shutter speed of 1/1000th of a second at f/8. The picture is pulling away to the right a little, and this could be corrected by a more careful look through the viewfinder or by subsequent trimming. There is, of course, no reason why the subjects should be absolutely in the centre of the picture. But if they are a bit off-centre in one direction, there needs to be something of interest in the other direction, to provide balance. The foliage to the right of the man does not really offer the interest that the eye is seeking. There's quite a lot of dead space at the top of the picture, too. It would have been possible to reduce this by bringing the camera closer. If the point were reached where there was insufficient room for two people to fit in side by side, it would be possible to change to landscape format. As it stands, this is a quite tolerable picture, but the people could have filled more of the space.

The rough surface of the wall provides a usefully textured but unassertive background for Figure 8. A lightning conductor grows from the head of the man on the right, but much movement of the group to the left would have brought a similarly awkward encounter with the drainpipe. It should have been possible to move them all across a little and bring the camera a shade closer to fit everybody between the items of wall furniture, which could perhaps be edged out of the picture completely. It is, of course, that ever-difficult subject, a group. Merely achieving a picture in which nobody blinks or pulls a face is something of an achievement when so many people are involved. There is a way of increasing the chances of such an achievement when faced with a group. You simply take more than one shot. After all, one shot requires a 100% success rate, while two shots need a success rate of only 50%. On this occasion several photos were taken. Notice the grouping. It is close to the traditional standing-in-a-row formula, but turns out, on closer examination, to be something a bit more interesting than that. The two shortest children have been brought forward, each in front of its mother, and the remaining figures have been arranged with the tallest on the outsides so that there is a curved line of heads. The visual symmetry, by which each group of four is a rough mirror version of the other, is echoed by a thematic symmetry, for this picture is of two families, the dividing line between them is in the centre, and

Figure 7

Figure 8

father, mother and children of one family are each balanced by their counterpart from the other.

With Figure 9 we move on to scenery and a picture of a kind that I seem to recall specialising in when I had my first camera. The view is of a park, but all the interesting details are away in the distance. The vast and featureless foreground is relieved by nothing more exciting than a bald patch on the grass. The sloping horizon is what happens when a snatched shot is taken without looking carefully through the viewfinder. The pale and featureless sky was a relentless fact of life during the period when the illustrations for this book were taken. Coloured filters placed over the lens can alter the look of sky, but no such subterfuge was attempted here, or in the pictures which follow. In some subsequent shots the blank sky is broken up or used as contrast. In this example it does rather take over. The sad thing is that a much better shot was on offer.

That shot appears as Figure 10. It has taken very little to produce this markedly different effect. The photographer simply turned through about 45°, and the view was there for the taking. The line of trees recedes from the foreground and gives a sense of depth to the picture. The network of branches breaks up and stands out against the white sky. The camera has been turned to give portrait format, which emphasises the height of the trees and narrows the amount of grassy foreground that we see. It is altogether much better. Actually, as well as turning a little, the photographer also moved a step or two to one side, in order to cut a sign and a litter bin out of the right side of the picture. A lone figure can be seen walking along the path on the far side of the trees. A few more seconds would have seen it disappear. A craft knife now could, if wished, do the job that a few seconds didn't do then.

Figure 11 shows the north side of a church. It is quite imposing, it is balanced by the pillared entrance to the building across the street, and another mediaeval tower can be made out in the distance. The scattering of human beings is not too off-putting, but the same can't be said for the cars. Two of these are on the move, though the shutter speed of 1/1000th of a second has frozen their motion. A little patience would have seen them out of the way, though by that time more might have taken their place. Patience would eventually, though, have been rewarded with a street free of moving traffic. But the parked cars would still be there, and that situation would probably remain much the same until dark. Additional unloveliness is provided by the very modern street light and the car park's ticket machine close to it. There is a slight parallax effect, seen in the converging tendencies of pillars to the left and tower to the right, but expensive angle-correcting equipment or a first floor viewpoint would be needed to avoid this. Parallax is something that often has to be accepted. The effect would be increased if the camera were tilted slightly up to get in less foreground and more church tower.

Figure 9

Figure 10

Figure 11

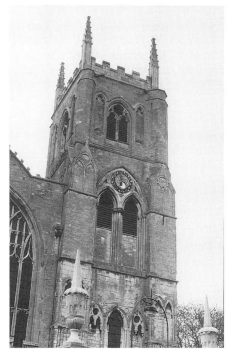

Figure 12

One solution is shown by Figure 12. The photographer has crossed to the west front of the church and concentrated on one of the twin towers. Cars and street furniture have been lost, and the eye can concentrate on the building itself. The parallax effect is evident on what can be seen of the west window, but it quite pleasantly accentuates the height of the tower. The blandness of the sky may be a pity, but the architectural detail loses nothing by the contrast. One feature of the photographer's task was limited time. She did not have the luxury of waiting long for different weather or of trying several shots over an extended period. She was put in the position of a family historian making a fairly brief visit to an ancestral location, and had to make the best of the situation. Here she could have stopped the camera down a little to let less light in. The result would have been a sky that was less washed-out, but it would still have been a nondescript grey, and the building, which is well-lit in this picture, would have been darker. If there is a problem with light, the answer is to set the camera for the part of the view that matters most.

So, what do you do when confronted with the scene shown in Figure 13? There are one-way and no-left-turn signs at one end of the building and another street sign with its back to us at the other. A no-entry sign is partly visible on the building at the end of the street and a keep-clear instruction has been painted on the road itself. As a final flourish, a car has been parked outside. It's a lovely mediaeval building, the frame is well filled, and there is a good sense of depth, with the house fronts receding towards a further old building at the end of the view. One television aerial is visible, which is an agreeably low score, and it half loses itself against the sky. The house has had attention over the years, of course. The sash-cord windows, though old, are newer than their surroundings, and the nearer upstairs windows are more modern still. But replacement has been tackled sympathetically. The street is a conservation area, and even the colour of paint has to be approved. So I don't think we can complain about changes to the fabric. One price that historians have to pay for the preservation of such antiquities is that the present occupants should be permitted to protect themselves against draughts and rain. But the building is besieged by horrors (some of which, in regulating traffic flow, are helping to keep it in one piece). There are few options open to the photographer. A shot from the opposite direction would merely give a close-up of different street signs, and there are, indeed, further examples at the far end of the street which have been cut out by the present view. I think that, if I had any time at all, I would come back a little later in the hope that the parked car would have moved on. If I were in luck, I would then try this basic shot, but from a little closer, in order to cut out the road signs to the left of the picture. This end of the building would probably have to be sacrificed as well.

If the view of the ancestral home is partly blocked, it may at least be possible, as Figure 14 shows, to manage a clear shot of the ancestral street. This shot is taken from much the same place as the previous one, but looks the other way. Though

Figure 13

Figure 14

much the same, the standpoint is not identical, for the photographer has moved from the road to the pavement to avoid yet another parked car coming into view. It is worth pointing out, in passing, that, from the photographer's point of view, roads are there to be crossed or stood in, if that can improve the angle. A companion who will look out for coming traffic is sometimes a useful accessory. The side of the building on the left provides a useful frame, though, as frames go, drainpipes are not the most romantic. A degree of parallax has proved unavoidable.

It's back to church for Figure 15. This nineteenth century example is less attractive than the one previously used, but it would look better if it were more successfully lit. The picture shows why our forebears were so keen, though ill-advised, to have the subjects of their snaps squinting into the sun. Strong sunlight comes from behind the building and causes two unpleasant effects. The west front of the church is in shadow and, though some detail can be made out in the gloom, there is no direct light to model it. And the sunlight has actually caused flare around the right-hand turret, giving rise to the burnt-out effect of overexposure. The patch of tree, top right, is pleasant. So is the accidental detail of the bird on the central cross. But the picture of the church is disappointing, and something better could have been achieved.

And Figure 16 achieves it. It's the same church, but the photographer has walked around it and settled on a better angle. The church is still not especially picturesque, representing as it does a relatively restrained form of Victorian gothic. But it is much better lit, and something has been made of its setting on the edge of a park. We see the building through the line of trees, and they pretty the scene up in a way that is very welcome. The result is quite an appealing shot of a fairly unremarkable building. The result has been helped, too, by some thought about positioning the camera, for the setting is not quite as secluded as it looks. The church may be in a park, but it faces a busy road. Had the viewfinder been allowed to stray a little to the right it would have found a lamp post, a road sign and a constant stream of traffic.

Figure 17 appears to represent a return to pictures of people, and that is partly true. We are faced with a group photo of little distinction. One person has blinked at the key moment, and a second shot, which might have been better, was not taken. The camera is pointing a bit too far to the right. An off-centre subject is not an imprisonable offence, but it should ideally happen for a reason other than careless use of the viewfinder. The flash is reflected by four lenses. The wallpaper is not a very happy choice of background, especially since it demonstrates that you don't need a tall building to achieve a parallax effect. But, whilst all these points may be noticed, they are not the main reason for including the print. The picture is an example of photographing an object and has been made from a copy negative. The hand-held method was used, and the 1/1000th of a second exposure ensured that there would be no problem with camera shake. The aperture was set at f/5.6, a

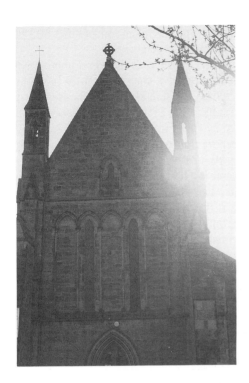

Figure 15

Figure 16

+2 dioptre close-up lens was fitted, and the picture was taken indoors in a well-lit area by a window. It may not be a good group, but it's a good copy.

It would come as no surprise to discover that Figure 18 is the worst photograph ever to be used as a book illustration. It is the second of the two pictures taken by an automatic 35mm compact camera which, it should be emphasised, is a distinguished example of its kind. The subject, as I trust can be discerned, is exactly the same as for Figure 17. It may be that I am labouring the point, but people are sometimes very reluctant to believe that only an SLR camera, suitably lensed, can handle close-up work. The compact camera's lens simply cannot focus down to such a close subject, and the outcome is a blur. The lens and viewfinder see from slightly different positions, so what looked fine in the viewfinder is not exactly what appears in the picture. The surface on which the original rested for copying makes an appearance at the right and bottom of this version, while the left hand member of the group has entirely disappeared from the frame. As a final malignant touch, the automatic camera has decided that flash is called for, and this has bounced back from the glossy surface of the original to give the white oblong to the right of the older woman's head. The recommendation of an SLR for close-up work is not photographer's snobbery. It's simply a question of what works.

With the sermonising over, we turn to Figure 19, and another example of a print from a copy negative. This time a smaller original, a Victorian carte de visite, has been copied, and the hand-held, natural light method with a +2 dioptre lens has again been used. Lighting conditions were less bright on this occasion, but even with an exposure of 1/60th of a second at f/2.8 it has been possible to keep the camera steady enough. This time some of the surface on which the carte was placed has been deliberately included. There are two reasons for this. It shows how the leather cover of an old book can make a pleasant background. But it also highlights a problem that can occur with the hand-held method. With a tripod you can also use a spirit level. With hand-holding you have to rely on the eye, and it is possible that the camera is not quite parallel to the surface of the print when the shutter is pressed. The result is a degree of distortion, and this can be seen here by noticing that the left hand edge of the carte is a little longer than the right hand edge. The sensible precaution against this occurrence is to line up and take each shot more than once, to increase the chances of an entirely satisfactory result. In fact, that was done on this occasion, but, to serve the purposes of the chapter, the more successful attempt was excluded.

Part of a monumental inscription serves as Figure 20 and concludes this sometimes bumpy photographic odyssey. A close-up lens, +1 dioptre this time, has been used to allow focus on the key words. A time has been chosen when light falls on the face of the stone, but somewhat from the side. So the surface is brightly lit, but shadows form in the incisions and legibility is ensured. Pick on a letter or two, the As and the W perhaps, and notice the pattern of dark and illuminated surfaces.

Figure 17

Figure 18

Figure 19

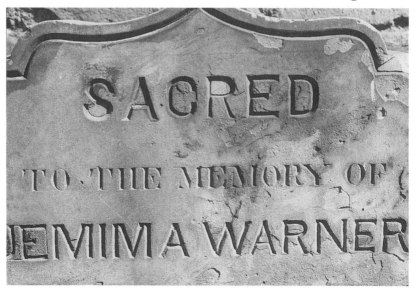

Figure 20

The top and bottom rows of letters are so deeply cut that something might be made of them at most times of day. But turn attention now to the Ms of the middle line, and to their left-hand vertical strokes in particular. These thin lines are unemphatic when dramatically lit; they would almost disappear if the light were directly from the front. One word of warning might aptly be added. If in the slightest doubt, allow a little extra space at the edges of the picture. It can always be trimmed off the eventual print. Otherwise the Jemimas of this world can come dangerously close to turning into Emimas.

Processing

Copying machines

Before looking at what the processor can do for the photographer, it is worth pausing briefly. Sometimes a photograph is not the only answer. It has already been suggested that a photocopy, supplemented by a close-up photograph of any key detail, might be the best way of dealing with a document. Photocopying can make a good job of reproducing paper items and can sometimes improve the contrast. Paper can be or become very brittle, and a photocopy can be worked with and handled instead of the fragile original.

The limitations of photocopies of photographs are plain to see, but they nevertheless have their place. They can be used as a sort of pictorial index, providing reference to a collection and reducing the amount of handling received by the genuine items. If you are preparing some kind of display, or mocking up an illustrated page, photocopies can serve as quite passable substitutes. I have found them useful for everyday reference when using old photographs as book illustrations. If you wish to record the backs of the mounts of old photographs, to save on the future wear and tear involved in removing the originals from a family album, photocopying will be cheaper than photography. It will give perfectly acceptable results in most cases, though the gold or white printing on very dark mounts of the 1890s may not reproduce well. Lastly, there are times when you wish to pass an old photo around the family for comment and suggested identification. Photocopying may be of service here, allowing you to retain the original, and letting you consult more than one member of the family at a time.

An attraction of photocopying to some will be the fact that they already have access to a machine. Being able to operate the machine yourself, adjusting the tone and having more than one try, is certainly an advantage. If you pay for photocopies at a shop, it might be worth asking yourself which of the possible shops is likely to have the better maintained and more up-to-date machine. Only experiment or local recommendation can confirm your judgement, but you may find it is worth paying a few pence more to get a better quality of copy. Good copiers can also enlarge (or reduce) your original, and this may be useful.

Laser copiers can also enlarge and reduce. If photocopies can often be surprisingly good, laser copies can be surprisingly better. They generally cost more and, like photocopies, they are on thinner and less durable paper than real photographs. But the quality of prints from a laser copier is very good. They preserve much of the sort of detail that is lost in ordinary copying, and they can cope with the subtlety of different shades of grey. When dating people's photographs I encourage them to send good copies rather than originals, and I find laser prints entirely acceptable. Laser copying also gives pretty good colour reproduction, though it helps if you can find a scrupulous operator, who will not charge you for any prints that may be wasted in the process of getting the colour right.

Whilst laser copiers are less easy to find than ordinary photocopiers, they are not exactly rare. Some readers will already have access to one. Others may find one in a high street photo-lab or print shop. I have been well served by one operated at the shop of a local telephone dealer.

It is a good idea to be aware of the possibilities of copying machines, but much more important to the photographer is, of course, the photographic processor, and it is in that direction that we turn next.

The basic service

Whilst the photographer has no need to know how the processing works, it is no bad thing to have some idea of what is involved and what can be offered. The first question is which processor to use. I am not, of course, about to make a specific recommendation, but it is possible to review the options. With slides you simply do what is required for that particular film, and that generally means putting it in the envelope provided and sending it to the company's laboratory. With prints, however, you have a choice. You can use a postal service; or you can take your film to a shop which sends it away and has the pictures ready for you to collect at an agreed future time; or you can go to one of the quick processing shops whose staff develop and print on the premises.

The postal service is usually the cheapest, extra prints may be offered, and there may be the inducement of a free film. The free film may not bear a famous name, but, just as with own-brand goods at the supermarket, the manufacturer may actually be quite well known. Many people are happy with the results.

Using a shop which sends the film away may not be much more expensive. The processing is done at large laboratories who arrange for regular collection of films and delivery of photos. Since this is often carried out on a daily basis, it is frequently possible to collect your pictures next day, and the system is therefore often quicker than the postal service. A free film is often involved here too. You may wonder whether to use the delivery and collection processing available at your local chemist or to go for the one arranged at a camera shop. The specialist nature of the camera shop may be a red herring, for it is quite possible that both retailers are served by the same processing laboratory. You pay a little more and wait a little longer, and, once again, most customers are satisfied.

If you use a high street processing lab, you pay more and wait for a shorter time. A one hour service is commonly offered, though you can usually qualify for a cheaper rate if you are prepared to wait longer. This kind of outlet, too, may sometimes run promotional offers. The hour service is very convenient, since delivery and collection can be slipped in at either end of the same shopping trip. Photographers are not great ones for deferred gratification, so the appeal of such a service is not hard to understand. Nor is it hard to understand that you are going to be charged a premium for it. But the extra cost is not just for pandering to your impatience. You get to deal with the people who actually do the processing, you can look at the results in the shop, and problems can be put right quickly. With the best will in the world, processors cannot always know exactly how a picture should come out, whether the darker or lighter parts of a picture are important to you, or whether the sky was really that improbable shade of blue on that day. They sometimes have to use their judgement. If they have erred, they should be willing to try again, and that is not the kind of service you can get when films are handled at another site. Do be prepared to believe, though, that there are times when their best efforts fail to wring perfection from a poor negative.

It may be instructive to follow, briefly, what happens to a film once it is in a modern laboratory. Whilst this will cover what some readers have no need to know, it may help others, particularly those who decide to cultivate a relationship with an on-site processor, to ask appropriate questions and to assess the service they receive. There are, of course, variations in procedures and in machines used, so what we are looking at is the processing in a notional 'average' lab.

Your film is loaded in dark conditions into a processing machine for developing. A complete darkroom is not necessary, so there is no need to be alarmed by the full lighting in a high street lab. The necessary blackout is achieved inside the equipment where the operations take place. The film emerges from the other end as a long strip of negatives which are then transferred to a printing machine.

The operator can programme the printing machine to allow for the make and speed of film and, in the case of 35mm film at least, can set it to print to the required size. The subsequent printing can be fully automatic, but, at this stage, the good processor will analyse each negative and decide how it should be printed. It is possible to add or take out some density and to make adjustments to correct apparent colour cast. Most of us find it hard to read colour negatives, but the practised eye can spot problems and try to allow for them. If such checking takes place, the pictures are printed one by one.

The customer generally has no way of knowing whether this kind of procedure is followed. We may suspect that often the technician simply presses a printing button marked 'N' for 'normal' and leaves the machine to work its way through the whole strip of negatives. At least, with the high-street lab, you can ask about their practice and can look through the results with a member of staff.

Once the prints emerge from the machine they are, or should be, graded. This includes checking for marks or dust spots. It may include the discovery that some are too light or too dark, or that some have a colour cast that was not detected at the negative stage. Such dissatisfaction may lead to a second go at printing certain negatives. This kind of attention to your photos is possible even within the time limits of a one hour service, though, at busy periods, putting matters right could lead to a few extra minutes being needed. (If asked to wait a little longer while some pictures are being reprinted, you should perhaps feel grateful for the care rather than impatient at the delay, though that may partly depend on how much parking time you have left.)

One other point should be made about printing machines. They do tend to cut out the very edge of a picture. Though customers only rarely notice this, it is a fact that may be worth being aware of.

So, what do you end up with at the end of the processing? A set of approximately 6" by 4" prints is standard, but larger sizes such as 7" by 5" or 8" by 6" can be asked for. If you think you will only want one or two of the pictures in the larger format, it will probably be cheaper to see the standard-size prints first and then order bigger reprints of those that you select. If you already know that you will want several in a larger size, it may be cheaper to have the whole set treated in the same way. If in doubt, ask about prices before you decide.

When you know that you will want a second copy of all or most of the pictures on a film, it will generally be cheaper to order a second set at the same time as the first. This is because quite generous rates are often available when two sets are printed at once. You can also be sure that the two sets will be exactly matched for colour and density, since the chemicals in the machine will produce slightly different results even a few hours later. It's rather like buying wallpaper: buy all you need at once from the same batch, in order to be sure of a perfect match.

The fact remains that you will often want reprints of a few shots only, and the ordering of these sometimes causes confusion. Negatives from 35mm film have a series of numbers below them: 1, 1A, 2, 2A, 3, 3A, and so on. The As have no special significance, but they do tend to make the customer feel insecure. To order a reprint of your chosen negative, simply quote the figure that appears most centrally below the image. If that includes an A, include the A when ordering. If two numbers appear under an image and they seem equidistant from the centre, you can always quote them both, asking for picture 13/13A or 26A/27. The numbering system is meant to simplify the unequivocal identification of a frame, but relating 72 different numbers to a 36 exposure film often ends up causing some uncertainty.

Other services

Various additional services are offered by processors, though even the high street photo-lab may not have the equipment needed to perform all of them on the premises. Selective enlargements can be made, which blow up only a chosen part of your picture and thereby give an opportunity to get rid of unwanted details that you were unable to avoid when taking the photo. Prints can be made from slides, though some loss of quality is common, especially where the original contains strong contrasts of light and shade. But a service which may be of particular use to some family historians is the making of copy negatives.

A copy negative is made from an existing photograph when the original negative is not available. Once you have a new negative, prints can be made as required. This, then, is the professional version of the close-up copying already described in the section on *Photographing objects*. It costs more than doing it yourself, but much less than buying a new SLR camera. It is, therefore, just what is required by family historians who don't fancy trying close-up work for themselves, or who lack the equipment to do so.

There is a possible complication though. Your camera shop or processor may decline to make or arrange for copies of professional portraits. Copyright applies, and it continues well beyond a photographer's death. In practice, few difficulties are likely to be encountered with the copying of obviously Victorian or Edwardian pictures, but modern studio portraits are likely to be rejected for copying unless there is some evidence that permission has been given by the original photographer. Individual processors may sometimes have an agreement with a local photographer or photographer's heir, whereby no objection is raised to the copying of the practitioner's reasonably old work. It is a situation where you may simply have to accept your processor's judgement. They, after all, are not trying to do themselves out of business if they can help it.

Prints from copy negatives are often very good, but there can sometimes be a loss of quality. The enlargement involved in printing up a 6" by 4" copy of a carte de visite, say, can accentuate any imperfection of original lens or focus.

Another piece of photographic technology that may be of interest to the family historian is the direct print-to-print machine, which can not only produce copies but also enhance or edit them. More than one such system exists, though the best known is probably the Digital Printing System (DPS), often referred to by its brand name of Kodak Image Magic. All machines of this kind can work from prints, and some are able to use negatives, slides or electronically stored sources.

Print-to-print machines have the advantage of being on-site installations, so you can enjoy service while you wait, and you do not need to surrender precious pictures for sending away. You can also view the proposed product on the screen before giving the go-ahead to print. The disadvantage is the cost. Systems may vary in expense, but none is likely to be very cheap.

For your money you can expect a reproduction of your original which reaches a quality that your own copying or the copy negative will not surpass. The print will be about A4 size (20cm by 30cm, to be more precise), and will be made on proper photographic paper. Therefore, although much the same size as a standard photocopy or laser copy, it is much more durable. But what is clever about the machine is what it can do to your image before putting it on the paper. It can zoom in to enlarge selectively, cutting out the passer-by who blundered in at the edge of the shot, or highlighting one person to extract a portrait from a group. It can alter the density and colour balance. It can add a decorative border, if you want one. As a useful corrective to a common weakness of flash pictures, it can reduce or even eliminate 'red-eye'. Then there is a choice as to how the space on the paper is used. You can have a full page-filling enlargement of your image, or you can have up to nine copies of smaller versions of it. You can have copies of it in assorted sizes. Or you can reproduce a collage of as many different pictures as you wish.

In short, print-to-print systems are versatile, and, if the cost of their use is compared to the estimated cost of achieving the same results by other methods, they may not always be as expensive as they seem at first glance.

A few miscellaneous processing services remain to be mentioned, and they are to be considered mainly as novelties. Your chosen photograph can be printed on a variety of objects such as mugs, T-shirts, jigsaws, key-rings, place mats, coasters and mouse mats. These may strike you as gimcrack gewgaws. Indeed, the notion of an ancestrally-illustrated mouse mat may make you wonder whether you were born into the wrong universe. But is it just possible that some kind of photographic novelty might serve as a souvenir of a family or one-name gathering?

Looking After the Archive

General care

Photographs really are remarkably robust. They survive being passed around, they are put in and taken out of albums, and they are often poorly stored. In spite of all this, they can last a long time, and the world is full of photos that are much older than any human being. Yet the fact is that they are at constant risk. They are vulnerable to light, heat, damp, dust, handling, storage materials and even their own composition. Light, both natural and artificial, can bleach them. Heat can make them curl and can dry them to brittleness. Damp can engender stains and moulds. Dust can be abrasive. Even gentle handling can take its toll, for the human skin is not chemically inert. Inappropriate storage materials can contain harmful substances. Even the photographs themselves are likely to have such suspect ingredients as paper, metal and assorted chemicals as part of their make-up, and these ingredients may be responsible for mottling, discoloration, rust spots, bloom and fading.

The solutions to the problems besetting pictures depend, of course, on the photographer. We each have to decide how careful and fussy we are prepared to be, and how careful and fussy we can afford to be. A little self-catechising may be necessary. Can I reasonably demand archival standards of myself? Can I meet the time-demands and expenses of a curator, or should I admit that keeping my fingers crossed is one of my main conservation tools? Am I a museum or a mouse? Speaking (or, perhaps, squeaking) for myself, I have to confess to something less than perfection in these matters, so I hesitate to prescribe to others. But the issues involved in caring for photographs are at least worth airing.

If nothing else, we can handle photographs carefully, holding them by the extreme edges, adding extra support from the back if necessary, and taking pains not to touch the image. Accidental fingerprints can be gently rubbed off with a clean, lint-free cloth. If an item is particularly precious, white cotton gloves from the chemist's shop might be considered for handling. And what goes for prints goes twice over for negatives, which are especially tender and scratchable. Since they normally come from the processor in sleeves, it seems wise to handle them in those sleeves as far as possible, only removing them for copying purposes or for transferring to a preferred storage environment.

Care over displaying is also fairly easy. If you want to put a photograph on the wall or sideboard, you can select a wall or angle which is not exposed to direct sunlight. If you need to be convinced that this is a good idea, you don't have to think of such lofty examples as illuminated manuscripts stored in dimly lit or heavily curtained museum cases. You have only to look at those old Penguin books on your shelves and to remember the shade of orange that the spines were when you bought them. There is, of course, one other thing you can do to protect a valuable picture from the light. You can make a copy and display that, leaving the original tucked darkly and safely away.

Sometimes there is the problem of what to do about damaged or deteriorating pictures. This is perhaps most likely to arise with old photos, but more recent ones can meet with accidents, and examples that have been poorly fixed or badly stored can show signs of decay surprisingly quickly. Certainly I have reason to accept that some of my own amateur efforts at processing are not as satisfactory as I once thought them. If you decide that first-aid is required, it is probably best to resist the temptation to have a go yourself. Torn photographs should not be mended with adhesive tape: it's better to just keep the two parts together than to risk inflicting further damage. Experiments with cleaning agents, even with apparently inoffensive water, should generally be avoided. Children have been known to show unnecessary resourcefulness in passing a rainy afternoon in the company of a shoe-box of snaps, so, for what it's worth, I pass on the theory that metal-polish wadding is good for removing ball-point ink. I tried scribbling with a series of pens on an unwanted print on modern photographic paper. It removed some inks without doing immediate visible harm to the emulsion. I am also assured that nail-polish remover, liberally applied, will deal with marks without damaging modern prints. But, this being a litigious age, I stress that I am not recommending either method. Invasive conservation involves risks and, if the picture in question is precious, probably calls for professional help.

Again, what you can do with a sick or dying photo is make a copy. In that way you will at least have a version of the picture in an arrested state, before it gets worse. Torn pieces can be set in place and copied as if whole. As for stains or discoloration, it may be worth making or printing the copy in black and white. The blemishes will not disappear, but they may not seem quite so glaring when they are translated into a tone that is in keeping with the overall colour scheme.

It will by now have become clear that copying is a useful conservation measure. Copies of anything that is deteriorating and copies for display purposes have already been touched on. There is another category of picture that benefits from copying, and that category is particularly the province of the family historian. Any picture that needs to be passed around relatives for identification or dating purposes, or in order to stimulate reminiscence, might appropriately be copied. After all, damaging a photograph is something of which many hands make light work.

Storage

It seems to me that any storage system has three possible functions. Firstly, it aims to provide protection. Next, it is designed to hold material in an organised way, so that it is more archive than heap. One implication of this is documentation, which will be mentioned in due course. The third function of a storage system is to enhance the collection's chances of survival. Safe protection and adequate documentation are, of course, themselves likely to promote survival, but there is, perhaps, more. The material needs to recommend itself to future generations. A clear feeling of order may go a long way to encouraging a descendant to keep and value the collection, though too complicated a method of referencing and cross-referencing may prove off-putting. Attractive presentation and accessibility of information may also prove useful. I suppose that my argument amounts to this: what has obviously been valued may stand a better chance in the future of being judged valuable.

Photographs can only survive socially, however, if they survive physically. We should therefore house them somewhere dry, somewhere moderately cool and free from varying extremes of temperature. They should be stored so as to protect them from light and dust. If they are to be kept upright rather than flat, they must be held firmly and closely together to prevent curling. But they also need to be kept inside something, and it is worth reviewing the possible threats to prints (and, incidentally, to negatives) when it comes to choosing storage materials.

Wood contains lignin, a stiffening substance present in the cell walls of woody tissue, and lignin may harm photographs. The newer the wood, the greater is the danger, so antique chests may be safer than modern cabinets. Paper made from wood also contains lignin, and once again age brings some lessening of the potential for harm, so a Victorian album may present fewer worries than today's scrapbook. Metal containers are safe, as long as they are enamelled rather than painted. Plastics are perplexing.

PVC is generally recognised as the villain of the piece, for the plasticisers used in its production can migrate to the surfaces it touches and it can generate acidic vapours which have a solvent effect. Cellulose acetates, if plasticised, behave in much the same way as PVC. Pure polythene and pure polypropylene are chemically inert, though polythene is visually rather dull and lacks the see-through clarity of some other forms of plastic. Polyester is generally regarded as safe and is in wide archival use.

The problem for most of us lies in identifying kinds of plastic. Are we certain that we can recognise PVC's reputedly acid smell? How do we know whether cellulose acetate is plasticised or whether polythene and polypropylene are pure? We have, I think, to rely on what the manufacturers tell us, and when the plastic used in a product is not identified we should probably assume the worst. Since polythene is likely to be less attractive for presentation purposes, we should put polyester or pure polypropylene at the top of the list, and we may have to turn to specialist suppliers to be sure that we are getting what we want. There are a number of companies that deal in archival quality storage materials, and a look through their catalogues will give a good idea of what is available. In picking out three such companies, I intend no sort of comment on any others. In describing their products, I aim to inform rather than to endorse.

Flash Foto Limited of 4 Parkmead, London, NW7 2JW, aims specifically at photographers and specialises in high grade polypropylene products. Standard storage pages are produced for use in loose-leaf binders and come in formats suited to slides, negatives and prints of all sizes up to 10" by 8". Heavy duty pages and card pages are available, along with titling insert systems. They also offer an 'Archive Kit' with index and label system, acid- and lignin-free storage envelopes, pure polythene sleeves for negatives, and safe filing boxes held together with safe glue. Their telephone number, at the time of writing, is 0181 959 4513.

Secol Limited of Howlett Way, Thetford, Norfolk, IP24 1HZ, may be contacted on 01842 752341. Their particular expertise lies in polyester products and they cater for a general archival market of which photographic storage is just one part. Again a selection of page formats is on offer, with a choice of designs to allow for either vertical filing in a binder or suspension filing in a cabinet or portable unit. They also have polyester storage sleeves in a wide range of sizes, together with boxes, binders, files, mounting strips and corners.

Perhaps the widest range of archival materials of all kinds is offered by Conservation Resources (UK) Limited of Units 1, 2 & 4 Pony Road, Horspath Industrial Estate, Cowley, Oxford, OX4 2RD, telephone 01865 747755. Lists lack stylishness, but a list is the only way to include mention of their drop-front print storage boxes, clam-shell print boxes, snapshot boxes, archival albums, cabinet and album storage sheets, and negative, transparency and glass plate storage boxes. To name but some. Materials used include lignin- and acid-free paper and board and high quality polypropylene and polyester.

Each of these firms produces a very informative catalogue and each responds quickly to a request for it. For any historian/photographer who is anxious to store photographs safely, a bit of a browse through their literature would be very instructive. The drawback (and when is there not one?) is, of course, cost. Archive-quality products cost more than products obtainable in the high street.

What can be afforded is an individual decision, and we may sometimes have to resolve that, for the foreseeable future, some or all of our collection will have to run the risks of relatively cheap storage. It may be that some selecting is necessary, whereby we choose to treat more kindly those pictures which most obviously deserve positive discrimination, by virtue of their fragility or their importance within the collection. Selection does not have to mean throwing away, though anybody who gets into the habit of taking photographs needs to learn to throw some away. What it amounts to is a sort of triage, where you give priority to those pictures that you could least afford to be without.

You may find yourself making decisions about negatives, too. There is a case for erring on the side of generosity when deciding their fate. It will be clear by now that lost negatives do not mean the end of the world, since copies can be made of prints. Nevertheless an original negative should offer the best chance of a good quality print. In practice, I suspect that old negatives are only occasionally sought out and reprinted, but occasionally may be enough to make their keeping worthwhile. I also suspect that they would be used for reprints a little more often if they could be found. Organised storing not only makes it easier to use them; it also makes them more likely to be used. Picking out some pictures (and perhaps some negatives) for more expensive storage may improve their safety. It may also and incidentally raise their importance-level in the eyes of descendants and thus help their chances of social survival as well.

Thoughts of future generations bring us back to the question of attractive storage. Can we think 'descendant psychology' and guess what sort of system will recommend itself to them and encourage them to treasure the collection? Storage on CD or video might seem worth considering, not least because we are told that electronic images can be preserved indefinitely. I certainly wouldn't wish to argue against electronic storage. But I would wish to remind the reader of the case for belt as well as braces. Photographs are fragile slips of paper or pieces of glass, and they have, in some cases, lasted for more than a century and a half. Videotapes and CDs are still a long way from any comparable achievement. Like everything else, they must have their imperfections. Scratch a CD and scratch a photograph. Which is more seriously damaged? I am quite happy to believe in the longevity of the electronically stored image, but beliefs can be mistaken. There is nothing to prevent the photographer from using traditional and modern storage methods side by side. Neither one invalidates the other. The proof of the pudding will be in the surviving and, with any luck, both systems will outlive their creator.

The other kind of storage system that deserves some discussion is the photograph album. It keeps pictures together in the chosen sequence, it is convenient to handle and look at, and there is usually room to add captions or labels. It can be leafed through without the sorting, shuffling and replacing that can be the by-product of a box filing system. There are, too, some human beings who feel that a book is a pleasing artefact in its own right, and more special than a box. What is more, the album is traditional. Our archive may already include some, and any that we fill would be continuing an established family practice. It would probably seem a pity to remove photos from existing old albums, for they, with their inscriptions in a possibly identifiable hand, are themselves a part of the collection. Any lignin content has probably had its chance by now to do its worst and, if there is no obvious cause to rescue prints from a clearly deteriorating or damaging environment, it might be best to leave the old pictures where they are.

Their ordering and grouping may be significant, and the album which contains them is itself something that has been passed down. To add to the series would be to maintain a tradition, and that may seem very attractive.

If albums are considered, the question of which sort immediately arises. Several kinds are readily available in any sizeable shopping centre.

Self-adhesive albums seemed wonderful when they first appeared on the market. You could arrange pictures with minimal fuss and no additional fixing medium, and they were held in place by the adhesive already on the board pages and by the covering sheet of plastic that was smoothed over the front. But we soon came to learn that the plastic sheets might tear when we tried to peel them away from the sticky pages to slip a picture in. Not quite so soon, but rather quickly nevertheless, we noticed some discoloration of pages, with the adhesive turning brownish-yellow, and we found that pictures could slip out of position. Perhaps surprisingly, these albums remain popular, and it is probably fair to say that the more expensive ones behave themselves for longer. But think about it. Plastic of an unidentified kind covers the face of the photo, while an adhesive with some stain potential grips it from behind. Nuff said?

Flip albums can be cheap and can hold a lot of photos in a small space. An album consists of a cover within which, on either side, are glued a series of overlapping, transparent, photo-sized sleeves, into each of which two pictures can be slipped, back to back. Labelling is not easy, since there is generally no room allowed for it. A separate index is the answer, or captioned strips of paper slid between sleeve and picture. The sleeves are made of plastic, and since it is not normally apparent what kind of plastic this is, the worst should be feared. The structure of flip albums means that only two pictures may be viewed at a time and that, if there is a mixture of landscape and portrait formats, the browser must constantly turn and re-turn the album through 90°. There is also a danger, perhaps more characteristic of cheaper versions, of sleeves becoming unstuck as the album fills up and becomes thicker, thus placing strain on those sleeves which, though glued to the inside cover, end up as middle pages. It is also not uncommon for the sleeves to split.

More satisfactory in many ways are the slip-in albums, with transparent, two-layered pages, with slits through which pictures can be inserted into the resulting pocket. An album may offer a mixture of portrait and landscape pockets, though no album can be expected to predict precisely the combination of formats that you will use and offer pockets in just the right proportion and sequence. Spaces for inserting labels are commonly provided. Again, of course, we are talking about plastic pages, with all their attendant uncertainties. But slip-in pages can be obtained in the safe plastics, polyester and polypropylene, from suppliers such as those already discussed. These are often designed for use with loose leaf albums, so that the photographer can choose pages with spaces appropriate to picture size, and can select an assortment likely to coincide with the mixture of portrait and landscape shots that is to be stored.

Finally there is the traditional paper-paged album, which allows any size and format of picture to be set in any order. Captions can be written on the page, though white or metallic ink is necessary if your preference is for black pages. Interleaving is very important, to ensure that photographs on opposite pages don't stick to each other. A traditional album feels more agreeably like a real book than any other kind and it offers the greatest freedom for imaginative presentation. But paper is paper, and we have established that paper is dangerous stuff. If you search the catalogues of archival suppliers, traditional albums of acid- and lignin-free paper can be found. They feature less prominently than those which use good quality plastic pages. And they are not cheap. So can ordinary paper pages be considered? Each photographer has to decide what risks to take with precious photographs. I can only say (and this is not a recommendation) that I would rather use non-archival paper than non-archival plastic. After all, many of us have seen gross deterioration in some plastic-paged albums in a very few years; and most of us, I imagine, have seen photographs that have survived pretty well in paper-paged albums since long before we were born.

If album storage is settled on for a part or all of the archive, there are one or two points to bear in mind.

For paper pages, fixing needs to be considered. Hinges which use genuinely water-soluble adhesive are sometimes recommended. But, if in doubt, avoid any system that involves adhesive touching the photograph. Think of the stains you have seen caused by adhesive tape and various kinds of glue. If you have no horror stories of your own, ask around. You will soon find someone who can tell a sad tale of the wrong sort of fixing used in scrapbook or album. ("When I am dead and opened, you shall find 'Cow Gum' lying in my heart.") Photo-corners are probably the best of the easily available solutions. The stickiness is kept turned away from the print, and whilst a little plastic touches corners of the picture, contact is minimal. If you are able to consider the products of an archival supplier, safe corners and fixing strips become possibilities.

The ordering and grouping of pictures in an album can add to or emphasise the coherence of the collection. Pictures may be grouped for contrast or to illustrate a theme. Chronological order may seem appropriate, or you may consider organising pictures by family group, linking siblings together or parents with children. There may be some mileage in juxtaposing pictures to show a family likeness, to show one person at different ages, or to show members of different generations when they had reached the same age. Wedding photos from different eras could be set together for comparison, as could images of childhood through the generations.

The visual impact is also worth considering, and this is where paper-paged albums offer the greatest flexibility. You can vary the formats, mixing or grouping landscape and portraits as you think fit. You can vary the position of prints on the page. A single picture on the page does not have to be in the dead centre. Two prints do not have to be lined up exactly side by side or above and below each other. Move the pictures about until they look right. It often helps, when placing the photos, to think in terms of the two-page spread of the opened album, for interleaving is rarely fully opaque and you tend to see through it to the page opposite the one you are admiring.

Don't overcrowd the pages, unless crowding is a deliberate part of the effect. Empty white (or black) space can set off an image very effectively. On the other hand, a montage can sometimes be very striking, with trimmed pictures fitted together into a busy jigsaw, though a montage can hard to fix without using adhesive on the back of no longer square-cornered prints.

Remember that prints can be trimmed down before they are placed in an album, and this gives a good opportunity for getting rid of unnecessary background detail that you couldn't contrive to lose when you took the photo. It is not always easy to achieve absolutely straight edges and square corners when trimming with scissors. Offices and print-rooms often have a guillotine or sliding trimmer and you may have access to one of these. Otherwise a really sharp craft knife and a rule can prove satisfactory. My own preference is for a rotary cutter and a transparent but gridded quilter's rule, which allows you to see just what you are doing, and which makes right angles easy.

The other aspect of album filling that needs to be mentioned is the writing or printing of captions or labels. You need to ensure that later generations can discover, and decipher, who and what the pictures are of. And that is the point at which a new topic claims attention.

Documentation

Family historians are not the sort of people who need to be convinced of the importance of documentation. Their own experience of handling information makes them quite capable of devising a satisfactory recording method for their photographs. In many cases their motivation is strengthened by a frustration at having inherited an under-informative set of pictures from the past. So the devising of a system can be left to the reader, and what emerges will probably relate, at least in part, to practices of coding and reference that are already used in existing records. Conventions already employed to identify generations, patrilines or individuals will simply be adapted or extended to deal with the photographic collection. Family historians can handle all that. It's what they are good at. This section will try, therefore, to know its place, and will confine itself to a few comments about aspects of documentation that apply specifically to photographs.

We need to decide just what are the details about a picture that we ought to record. Dedicated photographers may make a note of exposure, aperture, lens and film speed, but the family researcher has other priorities. We need to record what our descendants will want to know, and those are precisely the details that we wish our ancestors had recorded for us. The most obvious requirement is the identification of the subject. Who or what is being shown? Also wanted are details of place, date and occasion. A note of the year may suffice for date, though the nature of the occasion may call for something more precise. It may be of interest in the future to know who the photographer was. However extensive your own activities are, a family collection is likely to end up containing photographs by a variety of individuals, many of whom are themselves likely to be part of the family story. If a photograph is a copy, it could be as well to record the owner or location of the original. If a photograph is an old one which has now found its way into your keeping, you might choose to make a note of its source. If you had to consult an elderly relative in order to identify people appearing on an old picture, you may wish to add the name of whoever made the identification.

Notes on group photos need to sort out who is who. The convention of a list which follows along rows usually works well enough. Front row, from left to right, followed by middle row, and so on, is fine as long as rows are clearly defined. Sometimes, though, informal grouping can introduce some confusion. A numbered diagram often serves on such occasions. The simplest outline sketch of the grouping will be adequate. Indeed, it is surprising how eloquent and unambiguous identification by sketched blobs can be.

Whilst it is certainly true that the family historian will readily devise a system of record keeping, it has also to be acknowledged that the chosen form of storage will itself influence that system. Most kinds of albums allow for at least some information to be entered on the page. Files and boxes pose a choice between recording information on the back of a photograph or recording it separately. That separate recording may be on a piece of paper or card that is always kept with the picture, in the same sleeve or envelope. Or the details may be kept apart from the picture, perhaps as part of a reference list or card index.

I would be inclined to think twice before choosing to put information on the back of the print itself. A little thought about the known or potential staining capabilities of adhesive labels should be enough to discourage their use. Writing in ink presents problems. Some kinds refuse to dry on photographic paper. Some kinds may seep and bleed. Ball point pens engrave as they write, so that they leave traces of their use on the image side. It is possible to buy pens which will write satisfactorily on modern photographic paper, but whether they should be used is up to the individual. The usual advice about marking the back of photos is this: never add something that can't be removed. It is good advice, and it effectively cuts down the possible labelling devices to one, the 6B pencil. Only a very soft pencil will leave a legible mark while exerting the minimum of pressure, and only a very soft pencil can later be harmlessly rubbed out, should that become desirable. And even with a 6B pencil, it seems sensible to write as little as possible.

What might be considered on the back of a print, therefore, is a pencilled reference number which leads to fuller details recorded elsewhere. Convenience of use dictates that these details are kept very close to the photographs themselves.

Some sort of off-artefact recording system will also be necessary for negatives and slides. Reference numbers can be marked on the mount of slides. If there is a problem with finding a pen that will write on the plastic, an adhesive label would seem acceptable. After all, it will not come into contact with the image. Alternatively, a spot of liquid paper painted on a corner of the mount will, when dry, provide a better writing surface. Negatives, even more than prints, need to be carefully documented, because they are harder to read, as images. They are also much more vulnerable to handling, so they should be taken out of their sleeves as rarely as possible. Good records can minimise handling. Nothing can be written on the negative itself, but negatives do at least come ready numbered, and some sort of further identification can be written or stuck on the sleeve in which they live. Again, with both slides and negatives, brief reference to a more detailed source is all that is needed on mount or sleeve. As with prints, a separate record system must be kept alongside the slides or negatives it refers to, so that inconvenience of joint use is kept as small as possible.

With really old photographs, even minimal reference to a fuller source of information seems undesirable on the artefact itself. Individual pictures might be kept in suitably safe envelopes or sleeves on which identifying details are recorded. If the old photos are housed in an ancestral album, you will probably wish to make no markings on either pictures or their container. It is also good to reduce the number of times a photo is slotted in and out of its allotted space. All information about a picture can be transferred to a separate notebook or reference document. Write down everything that appears on the back of the mount, and anything on the front that will be hidden when the picture is in its proper place. Include exact name and address of the photographer's studio, describe the mount design, the colour of the card, the shape of the corners – anything that could cut down the need for subsequent removals. Each picture can then be identified in the notes by its place in the album, using such phrases as 'page 7, top', 'page 20, lower right' and so on. Since there will be no page numbers printed in the album, a rather laborious recounting will be needed to match up notes with image, but that is better than frequent handling of the actual photographs.

A last thought on documentation has to do with computers. You may very well wish to keep your records on disk. It's a reasonable enough idea. But do keep a hard-copy print-out as well. This not only satisfies a belt-and-braces sense of caution. It can also enable information to be kept alongside the pictures themselves, and this can sometimes make for the greater convenience of use that has already been recommended.

Looking to the Future

When equipment was discussed, digital cameras were mentioned, together with the claim that they represent the photography of the future. The claim is one that needs to be considered.

The history of photography is, of course, littered with the corpses of devices and processes for which much the same claim has been made. Some, like the daguerrotype, were of great importance in spite of being short-lived. Others, like disc film, never really made their mark. So a degree of scepticism is not unreasonable. Nevertheless, the advent of digital technology looks important, and the signs are that it should be taken seriously. A form of photography that dispenses with film and processing does, after all, demand attention.

Instead of film, the digital camera uses a memory. In theory there is no limit to the size of memory that is possible; in practice the cameras currently available tend to have the capacity to store between 30 and 120 images. They look fairly similar to other cameras and are handled in a comparable way, though the user is presented with an LCD screen display rather than a conventional viewfinder. When the memory is full, or before (since there is no need to wait until a film has been finished), the images can be downloaded to a PC. Downloading tends to involve an adapter, but details vary and improved systems are already evolving. Once in the computer the images can be edited, printed out or sent by e-mail.

Clearly, then, the claims made for the future of digital cameras have some substance. The technology is already being offered by some photographic processors to restore (which is to say, create a manipulated copy of) old and damaged photos. The cameras themselves are taking up significant space in the high street shops, and a number of glossy magazines devoted to their use have already appeared on the shelves. A toy version of the cameras is being marketed, the latest successor to Space Invaders and Cyber Pets, encouraging children to edit Daddy's head onto Fido's body. Digital photography is very firmly here.

So, what of the future?

Old technologies can be replaced very quickly, as we have seen in the case of vinyl records. But they can also prove persistent. Computers haven't yet done away with paper: as well as the tons of printouts they produce, they have generated an enormous number of books and magazines. But how will traditional photography fare? I suspect it will be quite a while a-dying. To use one of the new cameras you need not only the camera itself, but also a more-than-basically equipped PC, and a good enough printer. Thus, for the moment, their attractions depend not on whether you are an ardent photographer, but on whether you are an ardent newtechnophile. And the cameras are not particularly cheap, though they will doubtless become cheaper. At present I would estimate that the cost of one of the middle-price models would be recouped in the time that it takes you to use between 50 and 70 conventional films, choosing relatively inexpensive processing.

Also to be considered is the fact that many people find traditional photographs, on traditional photographic paper and in traditional albums, agreeable and convenient to handle. They may, therefore, like books and unlike vinyl records, prove quite resilient.

But whatever potential the old technology has to survive, the new technology seems certain to burgeon alongside it. So, as we teeter on the brink of the digital age, it may be worth considering its implications. For the processing industry they are alarming. But there are implications for family historians too. And these have to do with the manipulability of the digital image.

Camera have always been able to lie. By and large, with studio portraits and with family snaps we have known what is likely. A little touching up of blemishes or hiding of head supports was standard in Victorian pictures. A little trimming of a print or the use of a filter to improve the sky might be common now. It all amounts to nothing more than judicious selection or modest prettifying. With public pictures, however, we have learned to be more suspicious. We know that famous heads have been transplanted onto nude bodies and that politically discredited individuals have disappeared from later printings of news photos. But serious manipulation of the misleading kind has not been something one has had to worry about in ordinary family photos.

That is no longer the case. Even a child can now produce a picture of Aunt Mattie's head on a dinosaur's body. Manipulation can now be more than a little cosmetic touching up and removal of distracting background details. Future generations will, of course, suspect something is not quite right if they come across an ancestor as half-triceratops or a nude great-granny. But not all such manipulations will be easy to detect. What if it's just cousin Henry's head on Cousin Kevin's shoulders. Does it matter? And does it matter whether our descendants can't be quite sure that great-grandfather ever really visited the Taj Mahal, in front of which they see him depicted?

I'm not entirely sure of the answers, but I suspect some discussion would be appropriate. Questions about the reliability of images may have to be posed in a way that has not been necessary before. It may be that family historians who use digital technology should accompany the results with certificates of authenticity. It may be, too, that future generations will not be able to look at pictures of their ancestors with the same sense of confidence that we can look at pictures of ours.

In Place of a Bibliography

At this point, when all that matters has been said, a bibliography is customary. But bibliography is there none. There are two reasons for this.

Firstly, I would argue that there is more to be gained from looking at photographs than from reading about how to take them. You may possibly have found reading this book to be of some interest. But it is not, I'll warrant, the kind of experience you would wish to repeat ad infinitum. It's time, if not to get your hands dirty, at least to get your eye in and your shutter-release finger supple. And if more stimulus is needed, let it be the stimulus of photographs themselves.

Life throws up plenty of opportunities for looking at other people's pictures. When friends offer to show you the latest shots of their grandchildren or threaten you with their holiday snaps, why not show interest? Treat it as a chance to view photographs thoughtfully and to decide what is good and what isn't. If you think something works, decide why. If you think it a waste of good sunlight, consider just what its shortcomings are and how you would have avoided them. It need hardly be said that you are under no obligation to share your thoughts with the proud photographers. You are developing your own judgement. But that can be done in the privacy of your own mind, without feeling an obligation to deploy your wit as well. There is nothing unfair about it. You are simply exercising a critical faculty that you will also be bringing to bear on your own work.

If you find you are becoming a bit serious about using your camera, you can look further afield. As well as learning from the efforts of friends, you can try to learn from the work of the famous. Look at the output of those photographers of the past who managed to capture the feel of an age and something of the nature of their subjects. What they achieved in their time and place is perhaps not unlike what we would like to achieve in our present, as builders of the family picture archive. Rather than list specific books, I choose to name some individuals who are personal favourites. Not every photograph taken by every practitioner will prove to be of interest to family historians, but each produced a significant selection of work which now speaks of people in a context. A session in a library will produce examples of the work of most of these, as well as giving a chance to discover favourites of your own.

Sample, then, the capturing of people and place in Brassaï's pictures of 1930s Paris. Make comparison with Robert Doisneau's images from the same city in the 1940s and 1950s. Decide how far Julia Margaret Cameron succeeded in pinning down the essential character of neighbours, servants and literary and artistic lions around the 1860s. Consider how Dorothea Lange, and others working for the

USA's Farm Security Administration, got to visual grips with the Depression. Explore the sense of community in Frank Meadow Sutcliffe's pictures of fishing and farming folk in North Yorkshire in the late nineteenth and early twentieth centuries. Investigate Henri Cartier-Bresson's depiction of communities and places throughout the world from the 1930s on. Try looking at Paul Martin's seaside pictures of the 1890s. See what sort of job David Hill and John Adamson made of recording Edinburgh society and Newhaven fishermen as early as the 1840s. Weigh up Bill Brandt's reflections of class in 1930s London. Bump into other photographers, of other places and times, whom I should have included in my list. Perhaps learn; I hope, enjoy.

So, look at photographs. But also take some. The reason for taking them may, primarily, be to fill out the family's pictorial record. That is something worth doing, and is all part of trying to be a good ancestor. But photography need not simply be a duty. By getting better at it, you begin to find it a source of some pleasure. And there is, of course, only one really effective way of getting better at it. You have to do it. Practice may not make perfect, but it makes competent, and competence is not to be sneered at. The surest way to improve your photography is to take photographs.

That is the second reason for the lack of bibliography.